JORDANIAN–PALESTINIAN
RELATIONS: WHERE TO?

The Royal Institute of International Affairs is an independent body which promotes the rigorous study of international questions and does not express opinions of its own. The opinions expressed in this publication are the responsibility of the authors.

The Center for Palestine Research and Studies (CPRS) in Nablus was founded in March 1993 and established in response to the need for active Palestinian scholarship on issues related to Palestine. Independent of political factions, CPRS serves as a forum for meetings of Palestinians and international researchers from various political backgrounds and ideologies in a free academic and professional atmosphere. Of particular relevance to this project, CPRS has been conducting public opinion polls on a regular basis, to record the reactions of Palestinians in the West Bank and Gaza to current political events. The polls provide credible scientific data and analysis with which to formulate policy options. Recently these polls have included specific questions on opinions and preferences regarding Jordanian–Palestinian relations.

The Center for Strategic Studies (CSS) at the University of Jordan was established in 1984 with the objective of conducting research in the fields of politics, economics, demography, the environment and military and security issues, especially in relation to Jordan and the region as a whole. In addition to conducting its own research and serving as a resource base on political, economic and demographic trends in Jordan and the surrounding region, the Center frequently holds conferences and seminars, bringing together international and leading local scholars and specialists. The CSS has also initiated a programme of polling opinion within Jordan, identifying attitudes in the Palestinian and East Bank or Jordanian communities towards each other and reactions across the board to current political issues.

JORDANIAN–PALESTINIAN RELATIONS: WHERE TO?

Four Scenarios for the Future

Mustafa Hamarneh, Rosemary Hollis
and Khalil Shikaki

THE ROYAL INSTITUTE OF
INTERNATIONAL AFFAIRS
Middle East Programme
in association with
CPRS and CSS

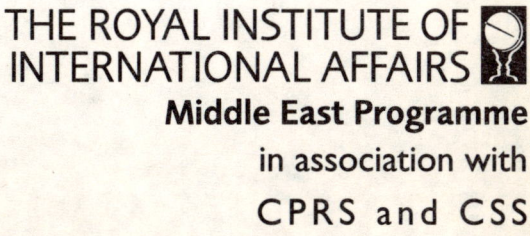

© Royal Institute of International Affairs, 1997

Published in Great Britain in 1997 by the Royal Institute of International Affairs,
Chatham House, 10 St James's Square, London SW1Y 4LE
(Charity Registration No. 208 223).

All rights reserved. No part of this publication may be reproduced, stored in a retrieval system, or transmitted by any other means without the prior written permission of the copyright holder. Please direct all inquiries to the publishers.

British Library Cataloguing in Publication Data
A CIP catalogue record for this book is available from the British Library.

ISBN 1 86203 002 2

Typeset by Koinonia Limited.
Printed and bound in Great Britain by Selwood Printing, Burgess Hill, W. Sussex.

CONTENTS

About the Authors	vii
List of Project Participants	viii
Preface	ix

1 Overview — 1
Introduction — 1
Facets of the relationship — 2
Contrasting perceptions and mutual suspicions — 3
The Israel-Jordan-Palestine triangle — 10
The regional and international context — 11
The Israeli–Palestinian dimension — 15
Entity-to-entity relations: four scenarios — 22

2 The *Drift* Scenario — 28
Contributory and countervailing forces — 29
  Leadership; political elites; political parties; the media; professional associations and other NGOs; public opinion; economic trends; the Israeli government; the international community and security measures
Implications — 45
Outcomes — 49

3 The *Functional* Scenario — 52
Contributory and countervailing forces — 53
  Political dynamics in Israel; the Palestinian leadership; the Jordanian leadership; mutual suspicions; Palestinian political elites, factions and parties; Jordanian political elites, factions and parties; security; economic factors and security constraints; the regional and international setting
Implications — 70
Outcomes — 74

4	The *Separation* Scenario	**77**
	Contributory and countervailing forces	79
	Political leadership; political systems; political parties; elites; civil society; refugees; public opinion and the media; the Israel–Jordan–Palestine triange; economic factors; the regional and international setting	
	Implications	97
	Outcomes	99
5	The *Cooperation* Scenario	**102**
	Contributory and countervailing forces	103
	Political leadership; elites; political parties and public opinion; economic factors; the triangular dimension; the regional and international setting	
	Implications and outcomes	117
	Cooperation under present circumstances; coordination between two states; cooperation approaching merger (confederation, federation, unity)	
6	**Conclusions and Future Imperatives**	**124**

List of Maps and Tables:

Map 1:	The Jordan, Palestine, Israel area	xiii
Map 2:	The West Bank (with settlements and Arab population centres)	xiv
Map 3:	Oslo II map depicting Areas A, B and C	24
Map 4:	Simulation of the Beilin-Abu Mazen plan (unofficial)	25
Map 5:	Detail of Map 4	26
Map 6:	The Allon-Plus plan	27
Table 1:	Preferred form of 'unity' as expressed in opinion poll, 1995	109
Table 2:	Comparison of *Cooperation* scenarios between Jordanian and Palestinian states	122
Table 3:	Plausible combinations of Jordanian–Palestinian and Israeli–Palestinian scenarios	129

ABOUT THE AUTHORS

Dr Mustafa Hamarneh is the Director of the Center for Strategic Studies (CSS) at Jordan University and an associate professor of history. He received his PhD in history from Georgetown University in 1985, and he has taught at the universities of Georgetown and Maryland. He has written several studies on Jordanian civil society and headed his centre's project on 'Jordanian–Palestinian Relations: The Internal Dimension'. He is the editor of *The Arabs in World Strategies* (CSS, 1994).

Dr Rosemary Hollis is Head of the Middle East Programme at the Royal Institute of International Affairs (RIIA) in London. Prior to taking up this appointment in 1995, she spent five years as head of the Middle East Programme at the Royal United Services Institute for Defence Studies in London. During the 1980s, she taught at George Washington University in Washington DC, where she also gained her doctorate. The title of her doctoral thesis was *From Force to Finance: Britain's Adaptation to Decline in Selected Arab Gulf States 1965–1985*. Her research and writing has covered the foreign policies of the United States and European states in the Middle East, Arab–Israeli relations and Gulf security issues.

Dr Khalil Shikaki is an associate professor of Political Science at al-Najah National University in Nablus and the Director of Projects at the Center for Palestine Research and Studies (CPRS). He received his PhD in Political Science from Columbia University in 1985 and he has taught at the universities of South Florida, Wisconsin-Milwaukee, and Columbia. He has written several studies on Palestinian strategic and domestic issues, and is the author of *Transition to Democracy in Palestine: The Peace Process, National Reconstruction, and Elections* (CPRS, 1996).

LIST OF PROJECT PARTICIPANTS

Mahdi Abdul-Hadi, Head of the Palestinian Academic Society for the Study of International Affairs (PASSIA), Jerusalem.

Ziyad Abu Amr, Associate Professor, Department of Political Science, Birzeit University and independent member of the Palestinian Legislative Council.

Ibrahim Badran, Economist, businessman, formerly of Noor Al-Hussein Foundation and coordinator for Jordan in the peace process and Adviser to the Prime Minister in Jordan.

Laurie Brand, Associate Professor, School of International Relations, University of Southern California.

Mustafa Hamarneh, Director of the Center for Strategic Studies, University of Jordan, Amman.

George Hawatmeh, Editor-in-Chief, *The Jordan Times*.

Rosemary Hollis, Head, Middle East Programme at the Royal Institute of International Affairs, London.

Hani Hourani, Director of al-Urdanah Jadid, Amman.

Ghassan al-Khatib, Director of the Jerusalem Media and Communications Centre (JMCC) and Professor of Economic Development at Birzeit University.

Bassma Kodmani Darwish, Head of Middle Eastern Studies, Institut Français des Relations Internationales, Paris and Associate Professor, Military Academy of Saint-Cyr.

Yezid Sayigh, Assistant Director, Centre of International Studies, University of Cambridge.

Khalil Shikaki, Director of Projects, Center for Palestine Research and Studies, Nablus.

PREFACE

This work is the product of a joint project between the Center for Palestine Research and Studies (CPRS) in Nablus, the Center for Strategic Studies (CSS) of the University of Jordan in Amman and the Royal Institute of International Affairs (RIIA) in London. Conceived in 1995 and initiated in January 1996 under the joint leadership of Dr Khalil Shikaki of CPRS, Dr Mustafa Hamarneh of CSS and Dr Rosemary Hollis of RIIA, the project involved six workshops, bringing together specialists on Jordanian–Palestinian relations, principally from within the Jordanian and Palestinian communities, convened in London, Amman and Nablus, during the course of 1996 and early 1997.

The starting point for the project was the assumption that the dynamic of Jordanian–Palestinian relations had been transformed by the conclusion of the Oslo accords between Israel and the Palestine Liberation Organization (PLO) in 1993 and 1995, and the peace treaty between Israel and the Hashemite Kingdom of Jordan, signed in 1994. The way was opened for the emergence of a Palestinian entity in the West Bank and Gaza Strip, which could potentially attain independent statehood, but which cannot operate in isolation from either Israel or Jordan because of economic interdependence and the complex interconnections linking Palestinians across the three communities.

While the two sets of arrangements provided formal frameworks for the evolution of Israeli–Palestinian and Israeli–Jordanian relations, a similar structure has been lacking for the furtherance of Jordanian–Palestinian relations. The project undertaken by the CPRS, CSS and RIIA was designed to define the dynamic at work in the Jordanian–

Palestinian nexus in politico-strategic terms, within the context of the Arab–Israeli peace process, and to provide a framework for assessing future possibilities and options.

The first imperative of the project was to bring together Palestinians and Jordanians from the two communities to debate the issues at stake, compare views and pool their expertise. A core group of twelve relevant specialists, including the three coordinators of the project, agreed to participate in the endeavour, attend the workshops and prepare background material. At the inaugural meeting at the RIIA in London in March 1996, the participants discussed the concepts and goals of the project; reviewed existing source material, available data and related work in progress; discussed the political context and potential constraints on pursuit of the project; debated the historical background and perceptions affecting Jordanian–Palestinian relations and agreed an itinerary for future workshops.

The setting for the workshops then moved to the region, with the core participants and some guest experts meeting at the CSS in Amman in June 1996. The previous month had witnessed the election of a new Israeli government headed by Prime Minister Binyamin Netanyahu. Inevitably therefore, the opening proceedings of the workshop were dominated by discussions on the implications of this for the peace process. A briefing was also provided on the reactions of the Palestinian Authority to this turn of events and the implications for Jordan were discussed. From this point on each of the workshops incorporated a session devoted to developments in Israeli–Palestinian relations under the new Israeli leadership and the status of the peace process. This provision ensured that the focus of the project would not shift from its central purpose, namely Jordanian–Palestinian relations, while taking into account unfolding developments in the regional political setting. The workshop in June 1996 dealt with land and water issues in the context of Jordanian–Palestinian relations; trade and the Palestinian economy; trade and the Jordanian economy; infrastructure arrangements; political elites; and a guest presentation on Jordanian–Israeli economic relations.

The CPRS hosted the third workshop in Nablus in July 1996. On that occasion, in addition to reviewing regional developments and the peace prospects, the participants, together with guest experts, discussed political demography; refugees; poll data on Jordanian-Palestinian relations; the media in both Palestine and Jordan; political parties in both Palestine and Jordan; and civil society in both communities. When they next met, at the CSS in Amman in September 1996, the participants and their guests discussed the policies and roles of Israel, the United States, Europe and other Arab states, as they affected Jordanian–Palestinian relations. There were also two sessions on security issues. By this point a substantial body of material had been collected and collated on key facets of the relationship under examination. This groundwork laid the path for a new departure in the fifth workshop.

It was decided at this stage in the project that something more substantial could be produced than simply an appraisal of various facets of contemporary Jordanian–Palestinian relations, to be published for the benefit of academics and other interested parties. From the outset, it had been clear that to arrive at a set of policy recommendations would require a higher level of agreement between the participants in the project on political objectives than was easily attainable. Consequently, the participants in the project redirected their efforts to formulating four possible scenarios for the future of Jordanian–Palestinian relations, drawing on all the material amassed hitherto. The four scenarios in question naturally presented themselves on the basis of the work completed. The names assigned to the four were as follows: *Drift, The Functional Scenario, Separation* and *Cooperation*. In each case these terms pertain to Jordanian–Palestinian relations, not the Arab–Israeli peace process overall or Israeli–Palestinian relations.

For the fifth workshop participants returned to the CPRS in Nablus in December 1996, having all undertaken preparatory work in the interim with colleagues, some of whom could not attend the Nablus meeting. This workshop took the form of a brainstorming, with the participants debating the feasibility of each of the four scenarios, identifying the forces which would be likely to help or hinder their realization and discussing the implications. It was a stimulating conclusion to a year of concerted effort by all involved.

The task then was to assemble the collective findings of the project into publishable form. With this in view, the three coordinators of the project, Khalil Shikaki, Rosemary Hollis and Mustafa Hamarneh, used the sixth and final workshop at the RIIA in London in March 1997 to begin drafting, between them, the document which follows here. They decided to rework all the material collected in the early stages of the project into the four scenarios devised in the latter stages. The result is therefore authored by the three coordinators, who must bear sole responsibility for the licence they have taken with the work produced, discussed and refined by all the project participants. As far as possible, every effort has been made to incorporate the valuable insights and data contributed by everyone involved. This is not a standard project report, however, in that it takes the product of all the working papers and workshop presentations, discussions and debates and develops it a stage further.

Thus, the authors of this volume are responsible for the finished product, but it is the outcome of the efforts, insights, engagement, endurance and goodwill of all the project participants listed here, not all of whom may choose to identify with the resulting compilation. The authors would also like to thank the guest experts who contributed at various workshops and would like to mention in particular sociologist Dr Salim Tamari, economist Dr Hisham Awartani, General retired Mohammed Shiyyab, PLO executive member Dr Asa'ad Abdul Rahman, researcher Ms Farida Salfiti and research assistant Ms Alia Toukan. They would also like to express special thanks to their friend Dr Salim Nasr, a social scientist, for the invaluable support and guidance he gave to the study group. In addition, all those who participated in the project and the authors in particular are indebted to the staff of the CSS, CPRS and RIIA for their work behind the scenes.

November 1997

M.H.
R.H.
K.S.

Map 1: The Jordan, Palestine, Israel area

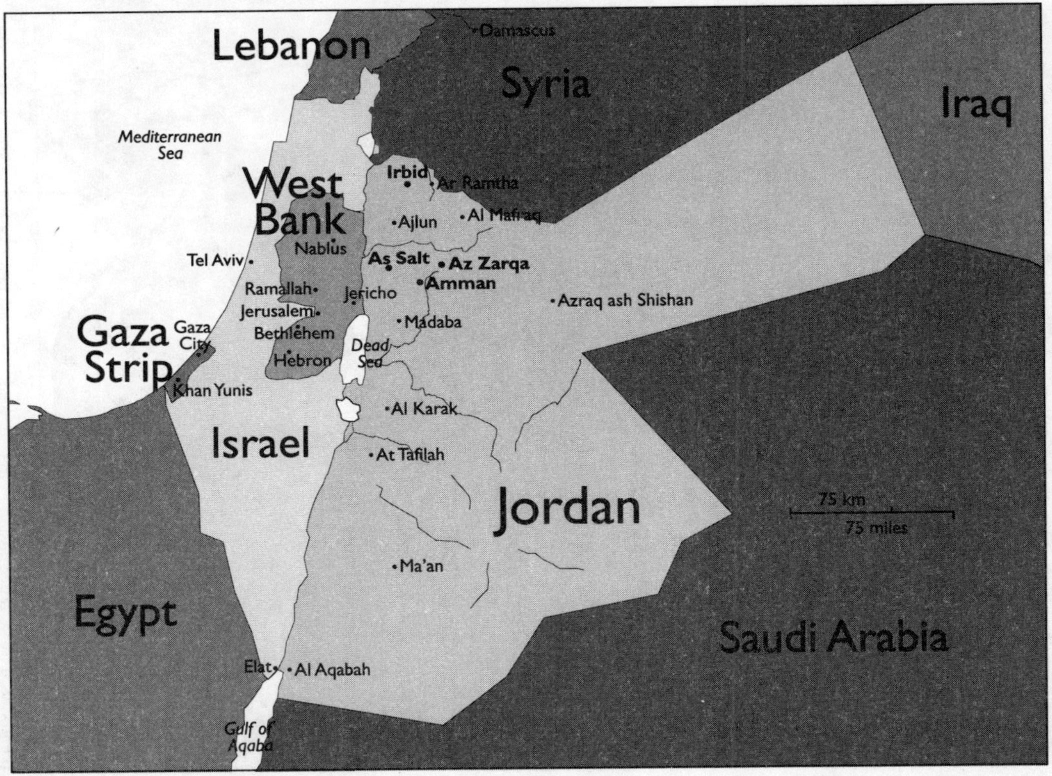

Map 2: West Bank

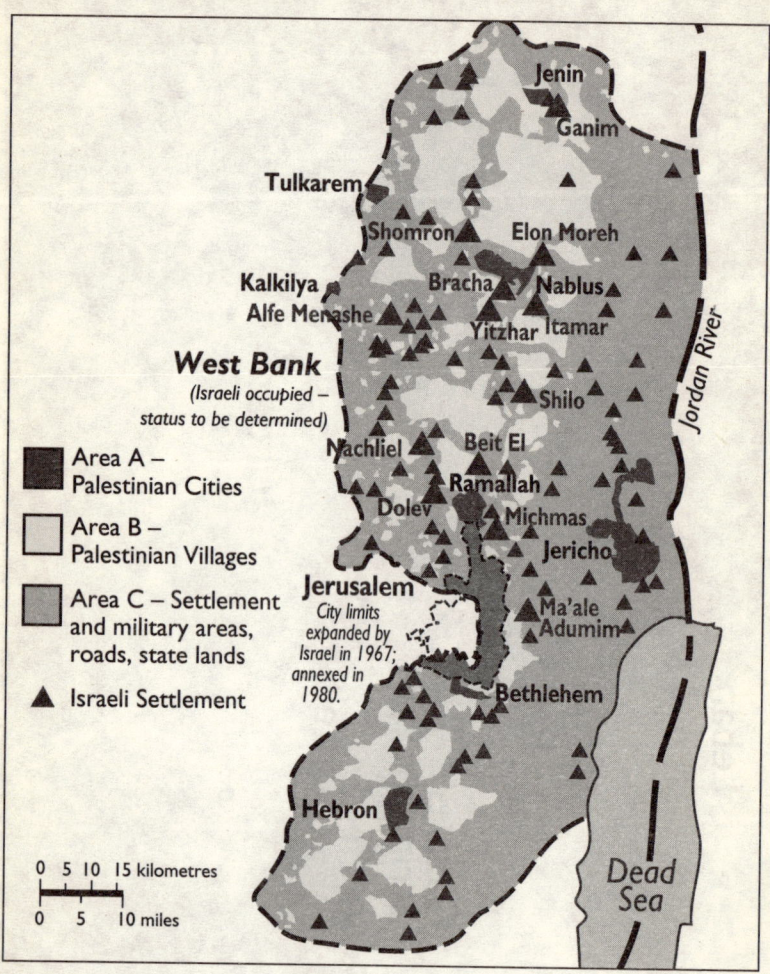

Reproduced by kind permission of the Foundation for Middle East Peace, Washington, DC.

1 OVERVIEW

Introduction

The focus of this study is Jordanian–Palestinian relations, a topic hitherto somewhat overshadowed by the broader issue of Arab–Israeli relations. The roots of the contemporary Jordanian–Palestinian relationship date back to the first quarter of the twentieth century, to the period of direct British and French involvement in the region and the historical process that led to the establishment of the state of Israel in 1948. Following the decision to amalgamate the West Bank with Jordan, formerly Transjordan, in 1950, the groundwork was laid for the integration of both banks of the Jordan, but that process was halted with the Israeli occupation of the West Bank in 1967. Yet, in parallel with new developments in relations between Jordanians and Palestinians across the river Jordan, on the East Bank the demographic composition of Jordan formed the setting for a further evolution in the relationship between the two peoples as a facet of domestic as well as regional politics.

The dynamic of Jordanian–Palestinian relations took a new turn when Israel and the Palestine Liberation Organization (PLO) signed the first Oslo accord in 1993 and the Hashemite Kingdom of Jordan reached its own bilateral agreement with Israel a year later. Oslo I, as it has become known, and the successor Oslo II accord of 1995, enabled the establishment of a Palestinian entity in the West Bank and Gaza Strip, which could be the makings of an independent state, but is nonetheless linked by history, economics, political, social and family ties to its neighbours in Israel and Jordan. Yet, within this triangle, while the Palestinians and the Jordanians conduct separate dealings with Israel on a bilateral basis, there is no parallel Jordanian–Palestinian understanding or structured dialogue. Instead, a general sense has prevailed that formalization of this relationship must await the conclusion of a final status agreement between Israel and the Palestinians.

The absence of a formal structure for Jordanian–Palestinian relations opens the way for events rather than policy decisions to dictate future possibilities. A number of crises punctuated progress in Israeli–Palestinian negotiations after Oslo II – notably the assassination of Israeli Prime Minister Yitzhak Rabin in November 1995 by an extremist Israeli opposed to the peace process; a series of suicide bomb attacks on Israelis by Palestinian extremists in the run-up to Israeli elections the following May; fundamental disagreements over measures taken by the incoming government of Likud leader Binyamin Netanyahu to reinforce Israeli control of East Jerusalem, and more suicide bombs in summer 1997. While the peace agreement with Jordan has all-party support in Israel, the Netanyahu government has never disguised its distaste for the Oslo formula for dealings with the Palestinians.

Under that formula, the Israelis have withdrawn their military presence from Palestinian population centres and are expected to progressively roll back their security presence in surrounding areas in the West Bank, while talks take place on how to settle the 'final status issues' of borders, Jewish settlements, Palestinian refugees, Jerusalem and water. Netanyahu has criticized the formula for conceding too much territorial reach to the Palestinians in advance of final status negotiations. However, he did agree to the overdue Israeli troop redeployment from parts of the city of Hebron in early 1997 and said he would agree to further minor redeployments elsewhere. This apparent concession on the principle, if not the spirit, of Oslo was rejected by the Palestinians as derisory and talks broke off altogether in March 1997 when Israel began a new Jewish settlement project called Har Homa on Jebel Abu Ghneim in East Jerusalem. In any case, Netanyahu suggested abandoning the Oslo concept of a transitional phase and moving ahead at once to negotiating a final deal. The Palestinian leadership held to the Oslo formula.

A new blow befell the peace process when Palestinian suicide bombers struck in West Jerusalem in July and again in September 1997. The Israeli government responded with the toughest security clampdown on Palestinian areas to date. Only US intercession managed to restart talks thereafter, though events were then to take a new and most unexpected turn following the capture in Jordan of two members of the Israeli secret service attempting to assassinate Khaled Meshaal, a prominent member of Hamas living in Amman. King Hussein was to extract a heavy price in recompense for this affront by the Israelis, including the release of Hamas scholar and spiritual leader Sheikh Ahmad Yassin from an Israeli jail. Meanwhile, Netanyahu held his first summit in months with Palestinian President Yasser Arafat. Nonetheless, disagreements persisted over the conditions under which Israeli–Palestinian negotiations could proceed.

The purpose of this study is to examine four possible scenarios for future Jordanian–Palestinian relations, depending on the actions and reactions of the parties to the Arab–Israeli peace process, and taking into account factors such as economic trends, land and water distribution, security concerns, public opinion and the roles of external actors. The rest of this chapter attempts to provide an overview of the current status of Jordanian–Palestinian relations.

Facets of the relationship

The Jordanian–Palestinian relationship is multi-faceted. It is a relationship between two peoples on either side of the river Jordan and beyond, between citizens and residents within Jordan, between two different entities on either side of the Jordan, between two leaderships and their respective governing bodies, and more.

The relationship between the two peoples permeates the contemporary debate about identity in Jordan. The way Palestinians living in Jordan identify themselves depends to some extent on the date of their arrival there, with those who came in 1948 considered the most assimilated. Yet this depiction may not take adequate account of the difference between refugee camp dwellers and others. In the light of the peace process, Palestinians in Jordan may be expected to weigh up the relative advantages of residence and citizenship in the kingdom depending on how the Jordanian economic and political climate evolves and, equally, how the Palestinian entity develops to the west. Palestinians on the West Bank will also judge the value of links to Jordan – and of Jordanian passports in particular – relative to what the Palestinian entity has to offer them.

The relationship between the two entities exists in parallel with the relationship between the two peoples and dates back to the separation between the two in the early twentieth century. In the recent past, however, certain milestones stand out against the backdrop of the Palestinian uprising or Intifada against the Israelis in the West Bank and Gaza and, more recently, the peace process. Jordan's disengagement from the West Bank in 1988, following the start of the Intifada, and subsequent elections to the Jordanian parliament (which dispensed with seats and votes for West Bankers), are markers pre-dating the peace process. Then, shortly after the opening of the Madrid peace conference in 1991, which the Palestinians initially attended under the Jordanian umbrella, came the separation of the Palestinian from the Jordanian negotiating team. In 1993 the Palestinians sprang their surprise breakthrough, with the Oslo accords. The signing of the Declaration of Principles (DOP) between the PLO and Israel, plus the Oslo II agreement, enabled the establishment of the Palestinian Authority (PA) in the West Bank and Gaza. Jordan meanwhile signed its own peace treaty with Israel. The Palestinian elections of January 1996 were a milestone in the institutionalization of the Palestinian entity and legitimization of its authority, and gave credence to expectations of Palestinian statehood.

Formal dealings between the Palestinian entity (hereafter also referred to as Palestine) and Jordan have taken place since the establishment of the PA much in the manner of state-to-state relations. Ceremonial and summit meetings between Palestinian President Yasser Arafat and King Hussein of Jordan for the most part follow the expected protocol for encounters between heads of state, no matter that their personal relations are known to be frosty. True, their various statements about their hopes and expectations for future relations between Jordan and Palestine have been somewhat ambiguous or evasive and the subject of much speculation. Yet it is clearly the case that the Jordanian–Palestinian relationship is increasingly about relations between two separate entities, based on two identities.

Taking it as read that the Palestinians are in the process of state-building, notwithstanding pitfalls and setbacks along the way, there are divisions within the Palestinian community on the question of whether and to what extent they should take into account long-term links with Jordan when deciding the shape of their prospective state. They have to decide now whether to preserve and enhance such links as already exist, whether to dismantle these and make a deliberate break with the past in the name of sovereignty, or whether to coordinate with Jordan as a partner in the creation of a wholly new cooperative and possibly confederal relationship. Without a vision of where they intend to end up, it is difficult for them to know how to proceed now, but judging by PA directives for drawing up wholly new bodies of law for Palestine, the current leadership appears headed for separation. The danger in proceeding without a clear goal is that others, not least Israel, may seek to impose an outcome, and it is worth remembering that the Palestinians entered their arrangement with Israel to establish their own 'self-government' without a clear idea of what this would mean. Ideally, the Palestinians and Jordanians will not be similarly ill-prepared to face their future relations and will neither drift nor be forced into 'confederation', 'separation', or any other type of arrangement with each other without forethought.

Concerning people-to-people relations, the Palestinians in Jordan certainly cannot be categorized as one bloc, in terms of how they identify themselves and define their preferences. Consequently, it is to be expected that, given a choice, some would opt for total assimilation into Jordan, others would wish to retain residence in Jordan as Palestinian nationals and yet others could choose relocation and citizenship in Palestine, circumstances permitting. Meanwhile, East Bankers or Transjordanians vary in their views on the options that can or should be made available to Palestinians in their midst, and in the extent to which they see their identity at risk as a result of the

Palestinian presence. The role of the Hashemites has recently become an issue for a small but vocal group of East Bankers who draw a distinction between the Hashemite royal family and both Palestinian and Transjordanian identities. To oversimplify, a three-way split has been depicted in Jordan between the Palestinians, the Transjordanians and the Hashemites, but individual, family and sectional loyalties and interests cut across this categorization.

With regard to a three-way split, however, a parallel can be drawn in the Palestinian entity, where the components are the West Bank, the Gaza Strip, and the leadership of Yasser Arafat and the PLO straddling the two. Gaza has an affinity with Egypt which distinguishes it from the West Bank, where the historical ties have been with Jordan. The role of the PLO, which embodies the national cause as well as the institutions, the leadership and the procedures which give expression to that cause, is crucial for maintaining the links between the two segments of the Palestinian entity. According to some commentators, though, certain PLO policies and the nature of Arafat's leadership style could actually work against forging closer institutional links capable of holding the two together. Others contend, however, that the sense of a common national identity is sufficiently strong between Gazan and West Bank Palestinians that, even if they may be temporarily divided, they will pull together ultimately.

Another factor to be borne in mind when defining Palestinian identity is the link between the heartland and the diaspora, 'insiders' and 'outsiders'. There are the Palestinian citizens of Israel, the refugees and some assimilated citizens in Lebanon and Syria, and those scattered elsewhere in the Arab world and beyond. These affect the Jordanian–Palestinian relationship not least because they have family links in Jordan as well as in the Palestinian entity, and, in the case of the refugees, if not others, they exist in a state of limbo pending finding a permanent home.

To sum up on the facets of Jordanian–Palestinian relations – the relations between the two peoples have to be considered in order to understand relations between the two different types of entity on either side of the river Jordan. After all, the relationship is a domestic as well as external issue for both entities, especially Jordan, where its definition is bound up with the question of national identity. A third element, relations between the two leaderships, headed by President Arafat and King Hussein, deserves attention since it cannot be subsumed under either of the other two. Lastly, as will be discussed below, the whole relationship has to be seen in its regional context, where Israel is the most important single player, but others, including the external powers, also have an impact.

Contrasting perceptions and mutual suspicions

The history of Jordanian–Palestinian relations is suffused with tension and misunderstanding. Mutual suspicion has been apparent not only between the leaders, but also between members of the two communities, across the Jordan and within Jordan. Some of the conspiracy theories on either side have been mirror images of one another.

The sensitivities of key players have influenced their judgment, affecting their actions and hence the whole relationship, often negatively. At the personal level, King Hussein is assumed not to trust Yasser Arafat and vice versa. The fact that they reached an agreement in 1985 on some sort of confederation cannot be taken to mean very much, given that neither has elaborated further on this since then and the regional context has changed significantly. On the Jordanian side, the lessons of the showdown in 1970 between the Jordanian state and the PLO, which was using Jordan as the base for its operations against Israel, carry a legacy. On the Palestinian side, the fear has existed that Jordan could aim to reclaim the West Bank for Jordan and not Palestine, though perceptions of the intentions of the Jordanian leadership have gone through positive and negative phases. Allegations of Hashemite collusion with the Israelis go back to King Abdullah's time in the 1940s and later there were the tales of secret meetings between King Hussein and Israeli interlocutors on certain occasions over the years. However, at the time of the 1990–91 Gulf war, Palestinian appreciation of the stance adopted by Jordan, and King Hussein in particular, marked a high point in relations. Thereafter, having entered the Madrid peace process together, the Jordanians and Palestinians suffered another setback in relations, with the shock to Jordan of learning that the PLO had reached its own deal with Israel in the secret Oslo talks.

Since the advent of the peace process a small group of hardline Jordanian nationalists has begun to make its voice heard in Jordan. Some of its members harbour their own suspicions of Hashemite dealings with the Israelis, on the grounds that the Hashemites have their own agenda, which is not necessarily about protecting specifically Transjordanian interests. One line of argument suggests that King Hussein, in pursuit of traditional Hashemite concerns such as responsibility for the Muslim holy sites in Jerusalem, will be persuaded by the Israelis and/or Americans to shoulder responsibilities for Palestinians in the West Bank as a price for retaining a role in Jerusalem. Transjordanian hardliners who fear this possibility foresee the danger of the destabilization of Jordan through involvement in Palestine. Others claim the king is not an unwitting tool of others, but rather that he is actively recruiting Palestinian support for his leadership on both sides of the Jordan. This suspicion has its counterpoint in Palestine, where the fear exists that the king may wish to prevent the emergence of independent Palestinian statehood on the West Bank.

Regardless of the king's intentions, real or imagined, a more general source of complaint among East Bankers is that private sector wealth in the Kingdom has become concentrated in the hands of the Palestinians there, who predominate in business and banking. Some also see the Palestinians as poised to reap the benefits of planned changes in the Jordanian economy and regional integration, while Transjordanians, working mostly in the public sector, will lose out. For their part, Palestinians in Jordan see East Bankers as receiving preferential treatment in recruitment to government posts, which also affords them a disproportionate presence in the armed forces and security apparatus.

The vexed question of national identity and citizenship also cuts both ways in the mutual suspicions of Jordanians and Palestinians. Transjordanians want to know where the loyalties of Palestinians living in Jordan lie. In some minds, granting Jordanian citizenship to

Palestinians resident in Jordan is no guarantee that their political affiliations will not remain across the river and, it is asked, could Palestinians in Jordan constitute a sort of fifth column? Among Palestinians themselves, there is some concern about whether they will ever be fully accepted in Jordan and how they are expected to fit in with the Jordanian concept of national identity.

Another area of contention has arisen over the activities of political and Islamic parties and groups across the Jordan. The Palestinian leadership has complained openly of Jordanian complicity in Islamist attempts to derail the peace process that have undermined the PA; and the presence of Islamist organizations in Jordan, linked into groups inside Palestine, remains an issue. Some commentators sense that the Jordanian leadership may fear the creation of a strong, independent Palestinian state, on the grounds that this could undermine Jordan's strength and stability. One Jordanian response to this, however, is that it would be more likely to benefit Jordan, by removing some of the pressure on it to accommodate Palestinians. Meanwhile, from a Palestinian perspective, there can be no peace for Jordan, or Israel for that matter, unless the Palestinians achieve statehood in the West Bank and Gaza. Anything short of that, and the Palestinians will resume confrontation and violence.

While not necessarily disagreeing with this view, there are Palestinians who foresee that the version of statehood they may be expected to settle for will be so circumscribed and weak as to be a state in name only. For those of this persuasion the idea that Jordan has anything to fear from a Palestinian state is laughable. In any case, both Palestinians and Jordanians are conscious that Israel will play a decisive role in determining what emerges. This assumption does not, however, make the Jordanians and Palestinians automatic allies. On the contrary, each side suspects the other of collusion with the Israelis in its own selfish interests. Consequently, one of the obstacles to Jordanian–Palestinian cooperation since Oslo has been competition for Israel's attention.

The Israel-Jordan-Palestine triangle

Both Jordan and Palestine figure in Israel's notion of its own 'strategic space'. In fact, it is probably more useful to think of all three existing within one shared strategic space. Within the triangle, Israel stands out as the strongest player, with the capacity to dominate the others and/or play 'spoiler' in their relationship. Certainly, Israel is not neutral and at the very least its ambition is to play the role of manager and balancer.

The Palestinians see themselves as the weakest entity in the triangle. Assuming they attain statehood, their sovereignty will probably be circumscribed and their economy cannot exist in isolation. Israel can determine the number of workers entering the country, can interfere in external trade relations and other forms of communication, and can also presumably still have a hand in the water supply arrangements. By comparison, Jordan is in a stronger position, yet, if the performance of the Jordanian economy does not permanently improve, the capacity of the state to take an active role in regional developments will be diminished. The anticipated peace dividend initially amounted to little more than some jet aircraft and other equipment for the Jordanian armed forces – which brought a new burden in terms of maintenance costs. By 1997 the need for something more beneficial to the people was acknowledged with the US decision to allocate $100 million of its annual foreign aid budget to Jordan, but this does not approach the 'peace dividends' allotted to Israel and Egypt since Camp David. Although macro-economic indicators for Jordan have shown substantial improvements since a programme of restructuring took hold in the mid-1990s, a lingering sense of *malaise* has persisted among the general populace and if this is not reversed the country could face social disruptions.

With the signing of peace agreements with Israel, Jordan as well as Palestine became beholden to that country for economic opportunities and trade. Israeli involvement in potash and fertilizer production on the Dead Sea provided one indication. After the peace treaty Jordanian merchants began to increase their dealings with Israelis, if only because their traditional markets in Iraq and Saudi Arabia had diminished since the 1990–91 Gulf war. Jordanian labourers have filtered illegally into Israel in search of work. Palestinian merchants, meanwhile, have long operated through Israel. Unless and until Jordan and Palestine find ways to improve their economic prospects independently, and cooperate rather than compete, Israel's ability to dictate to both could presumably grow. Even so, neither Jordan nor Palestine can be totally overruled by the other acting in collusion with Israel. No two of the players can ignore the role of the economy of the third. Also, in terms of sharing a strategic space, the Palestinians have a role to play in the protection of societal security, even if they do not feature in multinational arrangements and guarantees of state security.

In their own interests, coordination and a measure of cooperation, rather than competition, make sense for Jordan and Palestine, within the triangle. It seems most unlikely that this would ever extend to the formation of a bilateral bloc confronting Israel in economic or other affairs, but greater compatibility and complementarity between the Jordanian and Palestinian economies could serve to increase their relative strength and value in relation to Israel. Ultimately this could serve either to reinforce Palestinian separation from Israel or to lay the basis for more equitable dealings between them and Israel. Informal talks among experts have taken place to explore the feasibility of a Benelux-type arrangement balancing and integrating all three economies. Consequently, a range of possibilities exists, involving different levels of interaction between all three entities in the triangle, and the extent to which the Jordanians and/or the Palestinians will be able to mitigate Israel's comparative strength will depend, in part, on whether they can resist scoring off each other.

The regional and international context

Jordanian and Palestinian options and room for manoeuvre will obviously be affected by other Arab players in the region. If Syria and Lebanon remain outside the peace process, Jordan and Palestine may find themselves more closely locked in with the Israelis at the same time as coming under political pressures from outside. Egypt could play a constraining role, depending on how relations with Israel develop. Iran must also be taken into account and will certainly feature in Israeli thinking, as will Iraq, in Israel's perceptions of its strategic space. In this connection, Jordanians are conscious that the king's thinking includes calculations about his place in the region, as well as domestic considerations.

Egypt, Syria, Iraq and Saudi Arabia each have a sense of their place and importance in inter-Arab affairs and will interpret developments in Jordanian–Palestinian relations and their respective dealings with Israel accordingly. In Iraq, since the second Gulf war, the main preoccupation of the regime has been survival and thereafter resurgence. It can do little to influence Jordanian–Palestinian relations directly unless and until it re-enters regional affairs. However, underlying the ups and downs of government-to-government relations between Iraq and Jordan there are close ties between the peoples of the two countries which run deeper than purely commercial considerations. In Jordan the sanctions on Iraq are highly unpopular. In Israel, if not in Jordan, there are those who hold out the hope that eventually Arab–Israeli peace will extend through Jordan to Iraq. This may sound alarm bells for Syria, in so far as closer ties between Israel and Turkey could presage encirclement if Jordan and thence Iraq join the fold. Perhaps with this in mind, in summer 1997 Syria moved to reopen relations with Iraq.

For the duration of the present Iraqi regime the notion of a strategic alignment at the expense of Syria remains a long-term consideration. In the near term, though, any developments which appear to be leading in that direction will arouse suspicion in Damascus. Effective cooperation between Jordan and Palestine could be interpreted as such a development, as it could strengthen the position of both and thereby undercut Syria's regional position and weight. Relations between Syria and Jordan have always been tense at the leadership level, and between President Assad and Yasser Arafat there is no love lost at all. By contrast, President Mubarak of Egypt enjoys Arafat's high regard and confidence, which has enabled Egypt to mediate on the Palestinians' behalf in the peace negotiations with Israel. However, this amity will not translate into Egyptian support for closer Jordanian–Palestinian ties if these threaten to undercut Egypt's regional position by diminishing its role in Palestinian affairs and enhancing that of Jordan, possibly drawing the Palestinians into what the Egyptians sense could be an Israeli–Jordanian and even Turkish orbit.

The position of the Saudi government, meanwhile, will be influenced by its proprietary concerns about the Muslim holy sites in Jerusalem. The Saudis appear unwilling to give their blessing to Jordan as principal protector of these shrines. They could prefer Palestinian custodianship to that, but this presupposes Israeli acceptance of such an arrangement and in the near term the principal consideration is whether the Israelis can be persuaded to compromise their position on Jerusalem at all. Iranian declared opposition to the peace process is total on the grounds that it will yield no justice, but for practical purposes Iran's response to developments in Jordanian–Palestinian relations will be influenced by its relationship with Syria.

Broadly speaking, therefore, the regional context is not altogether favourable to closer Jordanian–Palestinian relations and cooperation, not to mention confederation. But, in any case, these relations are likely to be viewed as a subset of a much larger strategic picture in which the actions and objectives of the United States feature as key determinants of the attitudes of regional powers. Under the Clinton administration the United States has drawn a line between those states which are friendly and supportive of the peace process and those seen to be working against it, which also stand accused of support for terrorism and the acquisition of weapons of mass destruction. These latter have been dubbed the 'rogue states' by Washington and include Iraq, Iran, Libya and Sudan. According to its own policy formulation, the United States regards the containment of these rogue states as a facet of its support for the peace process and protection of Israeli security.

With regard to the peace negotiations between Israel and its neighbours, Washington's guiding principle has been security for Israel. The thesis is that Washington will support whatever deal the Israelis themselves can reach with the other parties. Publicly it has not indicated a favourite blueprint for future Israeli–Palestinian–Jordanian relations, and apparently it will not insist on adherence to international law, on Jerusalem or any other final status issue, if the parties themselves can agree on a formula. It has given its backing to the Oslo accords on this basis and has hoped to bolster the Palestinian economy as a necessary underpinning to the Oslo process. State Department officials have applied their efforts to overcoming specific obstacles to progress, and have refused to be distracted by arguments about the ultimate shape of a final settlement. Washington's approach to a breakdown in talks has been to urge the parties to return to negotiations, but overt pressure on Israel has been ruled out as counterproductive. When Madeleine Albright took over from Warren Christopher as Secretary of State in 1997, her initial response to the flagging peace process was to keep a distance, possibly as a way to oblige the parties to come up with something new to regain America's goodwill. However, by the summer of 1997, the situation had deteriorated to the point where she decided that Netanyahu's proposal of accelerated final status talks should be promoted after all, along with a call for what she called a 'time-out' or halt on settlement building.

At the time of writing, however, the United States has indicated no predetermined position on whether or not the Palestinians should have an independent state. Probably it would encourage Jordanian–Palestinian confederation, once there is more progress on the Israeli–Palestinian track. For the time being, Washington apparently does not see this as a priority worthy of effort. In the long run, it would probably see such an arrangement as in Israel's best interests. Jordan is viewed as a reliable ally and it would therefore seem preferable to link the Palestinians to Jordan, rather than have them on their own and potentially disruptive.

The position of the Europeans, by contrast, is that a viable settlement by definition should embody the principles of international law, and the European Union has come very close to stating outright its preference for Palestinian statehood. Beyond that, Europe appears inclined to encourage Jordanian–Palestinian cooperation. However, its leverage is limited, even though Europe is the leading donor to the

Palestinians and is engaged in signing up all the parties to the peace process in partnership agreements with the EU which will profoundly affect their economic fortunes in the future. Europe can encourage and cajole, but its influence is not decisive.

The Israeli–Palestinian dimension

Central to the dynamic of Jordanian–Palestinian relations is the question of what is to become of the West Bank, including East Jerusalem, in final status negotiations with Israel. The tendency in both Jordan and Palestine is to wait and see what Israel can be persuaded to deliver before determining their bilateral relationship with each other. Thus, developments on the Israeli–Palestinian track are generally accorded the status of an independent variable, while Jordanian–Palestinian relations are relegated to the status of dependent variable. In fact, of course, this is not wholly the case and the reverse could even be true. In this study the primary focus is on Jordanian–Palestinian relations, so developments on the Israeli–Palestinian negotiating track will be treated as both independent and dependent variables.

To prepare the ground for the scenario-building exercise, it is necessary at this point to outline possible outcomes for the West Bank and East Jerusalem, which incorporate the range of Israeli negotiating stances on final status issues that has been apparent since Oslo. These are:

(1) the Beilin-Abu Mazen Plan, which might otherwise be dubbed the '1967-Minus' solution;
(2) the 'Fifty-Fifty' solution, meaning a fifty-fifty percentage split of the West Bank between Israel and Palestine;
(3) 'Autonomy-Plus';
(4) breakdown and confusion.

(1) Beilin-Abu Mazen

The Beilin-Abu Mazen Plan is the term used for a formula worked out by Israeli Labour minister Yossi Beilin and Palestinian negotiator Abu

Mazen in 1996, which was allegedly ready for submission to Prime Minister Yitzhak Rabin for his assessment just at the moment when he was assassinated. The text has never been published or officially endorsed, but it has come to signify by repute a recipe for Palestinian statehood in up to 95 per cent of the West Bank and Gaza Strip, with Israel annexing the remainder. (Gaza represents about 5 per cent of the total area concerned and East Jerusalem 1.2 per cent.) Hence the alternative term '1967-Minus', since Israel would withdraw to just short of its pre-June 1967 borders. The land annexed to Israel would include four Jewish settlement blocs (see Maps 4 and 5). Palestinian citizenship would be extended to Jewish settlers remaining in areas under Palestinian sovereignty.

Under this plan Israel would recognize the state of Palestine and, according to sources familiar with the formula drawn up, 'both sides would continue to look favourably at the possibility of establishing a Jordanian–Palestinian confederation, to be agreed upon by the state of Palestine and the Hashemite Kingdom of Jordan'. The Palestinian state would be demilitarized and there would be a time-lag of up to ten years (up to 2007 as originally envisaged) before Israel would withdraw its forces from the whole area destined to come under Palestinian sovereignty, including the Jordan Valley. During this period Israel would continue to have military forces, early warning stations and air defence units in some locations in the West Bank and there would be joint Israeli–Palestinian security patrols along the river Jordan and Israeli–Palestinian borders. The possibility of a triangular arrangement for security in the Valley, involving Jordan as well as Israel and the Palestinians, is not ruled out. There would be an international observer force to monitor all activities and an Israeli–Palestinian coordinating committee to address all security-related concerns. There would be joint Israeli–Palestinian management of water resources. Control of airspace would belong exclusively to Israel above a certain height, and below this Palestine would have its own air space for civilian flights. Such flights could proceed freely between Gaza and Egypt and between the West Bank and Jordan, but Israeli clearance would be required for flights between Gaza and the West Bank.

The land encompassed by the Palestinian state in the West Bank, according to *Beilin-Abu Mazen*, would eventually form a contiguous whole with no Israeli communication corridors intersecting it. On the question of refugees, under *Beilin-Abu Mazen* Israel would acknowledge the 'right of return' to the Palestinian state and there would be compensation and rehabilitation for moral and material losses to refugees.[1] With respect to Jerusalem, the plan envisages a new 'City of Jerusalem' with two sub-municipalities, one Palestinian and one Israeli. In the new 'City' Abu Dis, al-Ayzariya and al-Ram would be included from the Palestinian sovereign side and would be part of the Palestinian sub-municipality, which would include all other Arab neighbourhoods in East Jerusalem. All Palestinians living within the Arab boroughs constituting the Palestinian sub-municipality would have Palestinian citizenship and be subject to Palestinian laws.

This formula is subject to contradictory interpretations, however. According to an informal Palestinian interpretation, not only would the municipal boundaries of the city be extended to encompass new Arab and Jewish areas (including Ma'ale Adumim) and a separate Palestinian municipality be created for Arab-inhabited parts of the city, but also:

- Jerusalem would be an open city accessible to all citizens of Palestine;
- the sovereign status of the city would remain in limbo until decided by a specially formed committee;
- it would be understood that the city would not be divided, but Arab parts of East Jerusalem would revert to Palestinian sovereignty eventually;
- the capital of the Palestinian state would be located within the expanded municipal boundaries and the Arab areas of the city would be linked to this administratively, functionally and in security terms;

---

1 Compensation for moral loss would be for each refugee family while compensation for material loss would be for each person with proven claim. Collective compensation would be provided for resettlement and rehabilitation of those living in refugee camps. Israel would continue to allow family reunification and would absorb Palestinian refugees in some cases, as proposed by an International Commission for Palestinian Refugees. This Commission would raise money for all compensation, rehabilitation and resettlement and Israel would establish a fund to contribute to its activities.

- the holy Muslim and Christian sites would come under Palestinian sovereignty.

Since the specifics are not fully spelled out in *Beilin-Abu Mazen*, it is open to a quite different Israeli interpretation, which is that, since the sovereignty issue is to be decided at a future date, in the meantime all Arab areas of Jerusalem would come under *de facto* Israeli sovereignty and by the time the joint committee had finished its deliberations or literally disappeared, over a period of years, it would be too late to reverse the practical realities.

(2) Fifty-Fifty Solution

The fifty-fifty formula is essentially a compromise on the *Beilin-Abu Mazen* plan. The Palestinians would get a state, but smaller and divided into three main parts in the West Bank, split by east–west Israeli corridors. There would be a fourth Palestinian enclave around Jericho. There would be no contiguous link between the Palestinian state areas and Arab neighbourhoods in East Jerusalem. Israel would retain control of military security in the Jordan Valley and, according to one version, the Valley would come under Israeli sovereignty. According to another interpretation, the Jordan Valley could eventually be handed over to the Palestinians, after perhaps twenty years. The powers of the Palestinian state would be circumscribed, in part *de facto* because of its division into separate enclaves. Also, there would be no contiguous border between Palestine and Jordan.

The *Fifty-Fifty Solution* is an extrapolation from various formulas or negotiating gambits posited by the Israelis since Oslo. It represents slightly less for the Palestinians than envisaged in a map produced by the Third Way Party. It embodies slightly more than the 40 per cent on offer to the Palestinians according to a map allegedly drawn up by the Israeli army and published in the Israeli daily *Ha'aretz* in May 1997.[2] It has some features in common with the 'Allon-Plus' idea

---

2 Patrick Cockburn, 'Secret map reveals Israel's West Bank plan', *The Independent*, 30 May 1997.

reportedly mooted by Prime Minister Netanyahu at around the same time.[3] (See Map 6) The purpose it serves here is as an encapsulation of a formula for statehood which would leave the Palestinians in isolated enclaves on the West Bank, disconnected from Jordan as well as from East Jerusalem. The implications for Jordanian–Palestinian relations of this outcome on the West Bank would clearly be different from the possibilities embodied in *Beilin-Abu Mazen*.

(3) Autonomy-Plus

If the Palestinians do not attain formal statehood, but the self-rule arrangements begun by Oslo are extended and regularized within specified areas, the result could be termed Autonomy-Plus. This is more or less what Netanyahu said he was prepared to grant at the time of his election in May 1996. The essential components of an *Autonomy-Plus* arrangement on the West Bank would be as follows:

- functional autonomy for the Palestinians over their civil affairs and internal security;
- no Palestinian army or heavy armour;
- maintenance of Israeli control over water;
- maintenance of an Israeli military presence in the Jordan Valley;
- maintenance of Israeli military surveillance arrangements on high ground;
- Israeli control of the air space;
- maintenance of Israeli settlements directly under Israeli sovereignty;
- maintenance of Israeli control of communication links.

---

3 The original Allon Plan, drawn up by Yigal Allon for the Labour government after Israel's capture of the West Bank in 1967, envisaged Israeli retention of some 30 per cent of the land, including the Jordan Valley, much of the Hebron Hills area and all of East Jerusalem and its environs. The Netanyahu notion of 'Allon-Plus' would apparently add on major settlement blocs subsequently built near the 1967 Israel–West Bank border or Green Line, bringing the total proportion of land for annexation closer to 50 per cent. See Herb Keinon, 'Allon-Plus – A rejected plan is resurrected', *Jerusalem Post*, 6 June 1997, and Shyam Bhatia, 'Israel's tougher stance sparks dire warnings', *The Guardian*, 5 June 1997.

The contrasts between this and the *Beilin-Abu Mazen* plan are clearly discernible. The *Fifty-Fifty Solution* constitutes something of a compromise between the two. The difference between *Fifty-Fifty* and *Autonomy-Plus* could be one of semantics. Netanyahu says he is set against the establishment of an independent Palestinian state *per se*, but claims that so too, in truth, are his Labour opponents, since what they would concede to a Palestinian state falls short of sovereign statehood in all but name. It is partly on this basis that he apparently claims for himself a role as peacemaker comparable to the late Menachem Begin, with the capacity to deliver a deal with the Palestinians that will have more broad-based popular support in Israel than anything that the Labour Party could produce.

Successive Israeli leaders Yitzhak Rabin, Shimon Peres and Binyamin Netanyahu are distinguishable in both their visions of peace and their negotiating styles. Rabin revealed more by his actions than his words. With respect to his Palestinian and Jordanian negotiating partners he displayed a personal dislike and distrust of Arafat and a deep bond of friendship and mutual respect with King Hussein. Yet the retrospective assessment of Rabin is that he became a convert to the logic of the Oslo process and thus the emergence of a Palestinian state in the West Bank and Gaza. He drew a distinction between Jewish settlements on the West Bank on the basis of security and ideology, indicating that those founded on purely ideological or religious-nationalist grounds could eventually be dispensed with, thereby arousing the enmity of 'Greater Israel' ideologues.

Peres, in contrast to Rabin, has talked and written expansively about his vision for peace, which is principally about regional interdependence and integration. Paradoxically, since he enjoys no personal rapport with King Hussein, Peres is associated with the idea of a so-called 'Jordanian option' for the future of the West Bank, rather than independent Palestinian statehood.

In both word and deed Netanyahu has been accused of giving mixed signals on the peace process. Having denounced Oslo, he nonetheless conceded redeployment from Hebron under the Oslo terms. Pressed by the Palestinians and the United States to proceed with a further roll-back of the Israeli presence in Palestinian areas, as envisaged by Oslo, he conceded on the principle but delivered virtually nothing in substance. Thus he proposed a small expansion of the so-called Area A, wherein Palestinians bear sole responsibility for internal security as well as civil administration, and a token increment in Area B, wherein security is under joint Israeli–Palestinian control. (At the time of this offer, in March 1997, Area A encompassed 4–5 per cent of the land of the West Bank; Area B about 23 per cent, and the remainder, including all Israeli settlements, remained under Israeli control as Area C. See Map 3.) The reaction to this offer was rejection by the Palestinian leadership and denunciation by hardline Israeli settlers.

On the issue of Jerusalem, Netanyahu has been less equivocal. Israeli sovereignty over the whole city is to remain undiluted. The decision in March 1997 to build the Har Homa settlement on Jebel Abu Ghneim brought Israeli–Palestinian negotiations to a halt, because of the implication that Palestinian aspirations for a capital within Eastern Jerusalem would be ruled out before final status negotiations had even got under way.

(4) Breakdown

Repeated and prolonged interruptions in negotiations could either spell *Breakdown* for the whole Israeli–Palestinian peace process – the fourth possibility in the range of outcomes posited here – or else open the way for Israel to halt the process at *de facto Autonomy-Plus*. The Palestinian leadership could not formally agree to *Autonomy-Plus* as a permanent solution. But if it cannot accept alternatives offered by Israel and the latter proves immovable, then the Palestinians may end up with *Autonomy-Plus* anyway. Fear of a total breakdown is meanwhile sufficiently strong to keep efforts at peace-making alive despite repeated setbacks. It is a spectre which hangs over all the parties to the Arab–Israeli peace process. Whether *Breakdown* means war on the Israeli–Palestinian front is open to question. More likely it means endemic low-level violence which, as will be explored further, has serious implications for Jordan.

Entity-to-entity relations: four scenarios

The foregoing provides the background to the main focus of this study, which is to explore in depth potential scenarios for the future shape of Jordanian–Palestinian relations. These scenarios were devised in the workshops that informed this study and are designed *not* as prescriptions for what should happen, but as tools of analysis. They provide a mechanism for comparing and contrasting different potential outcomes, in two to three years' time. They sketch what could transpire, depending on the actions and reactions of the parties to the whole Arab–Israeli peace process, and taking into account factors such as economic trends, land and water distribution, security concerns, public opinion and the roles of external actors.

Four possible scenarios for future Jordanian–Palestinian relations are offered here. The *Drift* scenario assumes that all the players involved, but particularly the Jordanian and Palestinian leaderships, fail to develop a deliberate strategy for moving the situation forward and simply react to events. The *Functional* scenario refers to the future status of the Palestinian entity and describes what could happen to Jordanian–Palestinian relations if a hardline Israeli government is in the driving seat and pushes forward with its vision of limited independence for the Palestinians, thereby barring the emergence of a fully independent state. The *Separation* scenario is what happens if Jordan and Palestine decide they want to develop along separate paths and acquire identities which are as distinct as possible. The *Cooperation* scenario means that Jordan and Palestine decide to work together closely to coordinate their policies and harmonize their economic, legal and educational systems and/or they decide to build some form of federation or confederation once Palestinian independence has been achieved.

The starting point for each of the four scenarios is the status quo in mid to late 1997. In other words, the relationship between the Jordanians and Palestinians, and between each of them and Israel, is as described in the foregoing discussion on the nature and facets of the relationship. Some thought is given to how any one of the four scenarios could come about. In the case of *Drift,* for example, it is assumed that the Israeli government does not act in accordance with a grand strategy any more than the Jordanian or Palestinian leaderships. All simply react to events as they occur and all are therefore essentially victims of circumstance. Under the *Functional* scenario, meanwhile, it has to be assumed that neither Jordan nor Palestine manages to seize the initiative for a sustained period, but a hardline Israeli government, possibly one led by Netanyahu, does. In the case of the *Separation* scenario, however, it has to be assumed that the Jordanians and Palestinians choose to go their separate ways, neither tries to impose itself on the other and Israel is not able, or does not attempt, to push them together. The *Cooperation* scenario can only come about if Jordan and Palestine overcome their worst fears and suspicions of each other, and third parties do not impede this.

The following four chapters will take each scenario in turn, offer an expanded definition of the scenario in question; discuss the forces most likely to lead to that outcome and those which appear to stand in the way; examine the implications; and relate the outcome to developments on the Israeli–Palestinian track.

Each chapter builds on the preceding one. The intention in Chapter 1 has been to set the scene for all that follows, but new material will be introduced in each of the subsequent chapters, with some background explanation in the first instance. The treatment of the various facets of Jordanian–Palestinian relations is not exactly the same for each scenario and only those factors which appear most relevant will be highlighted. Thus, while the discussion of each of the four scenarios is designed to be coherent and as complete as possible in each case, only by reading them in the order in which they appear here will the full picture unfold.

Map 3: Oslo II

Source: *Yediot Aharonot*, 6 October 1995
Reproduced by kind permission of the Foundation for Middle East Peace, Washington, DC.

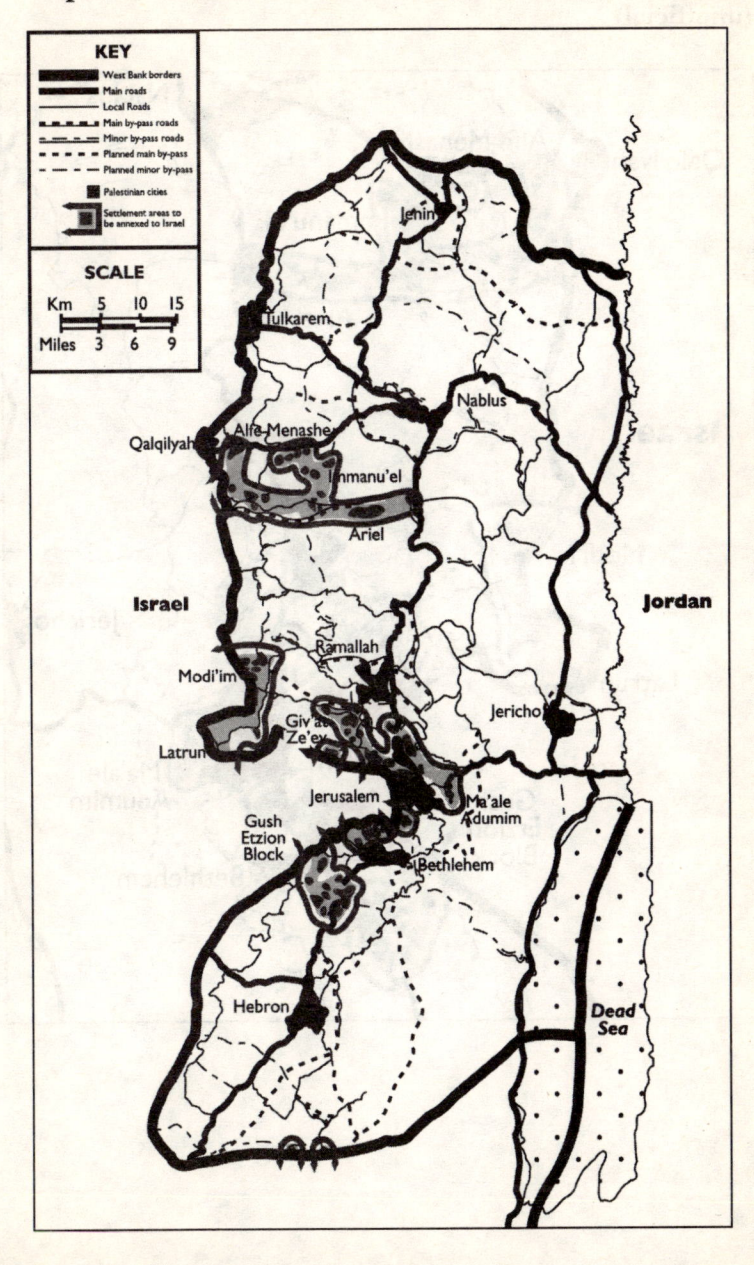

Map 4: Simulation of the Beilin-Abu Mazen (unofficial)

Map 5: Detail of Map 4: simulation of the Beilin–Abu Mazen (unofficial)

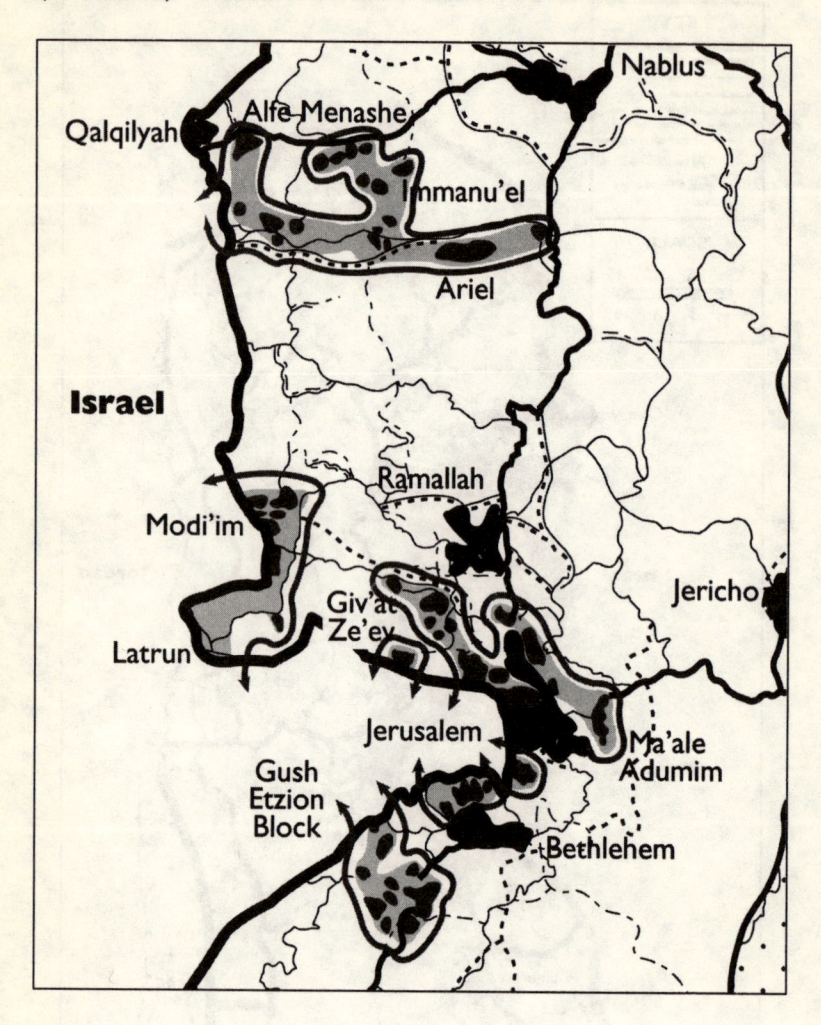

Map 6: The *Allon-Plus* plan

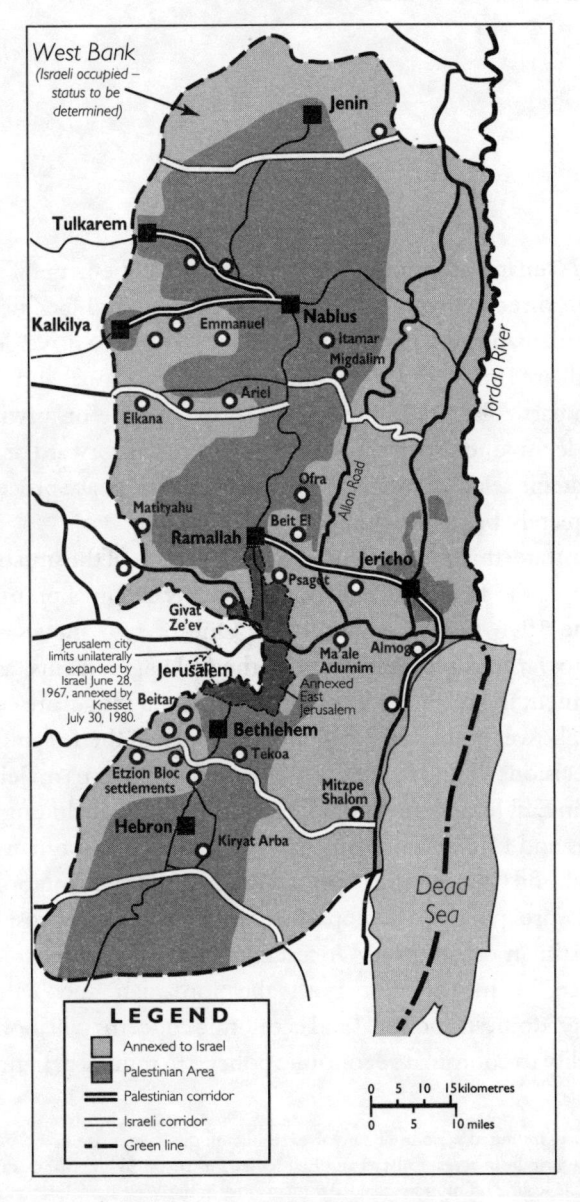

Reproduced by kind permission of the Foundation for Middle East Peace, Washington, DC.

2 THE *DRIFT* SCENARIO

The *Drift* scenario attempts to describe what could emerge if none of the players directly involved in the peace process, and specifically the Israeli, Jordanian and Palestinian leaderships, is able to drive developments. All are simply reactive. Similarly, other regional and external actors, in particular the United States, prove unable or unwilling to take any decisive actions to move the peace process forward or impose a new strategic relationship on the parties to it. The peace process need not completely break down, but it atrophies.

To illustrate, this scenario means a continuation of the situation that pertained in the first eighteen months of Netanyahu's premiership, from June 1996 to November 1997. One or two moves may be effected towards imple-mentation of the Oslo agreements, as in the redeployment in Hebron in February 1997. Such moves are counter-balanced, however, by unilateral measures such as the Israeli government's decision to build the new settlement of Har Homa on Jebel Abu Ghneim in East Jerusalem. Sporadic acts of violence, including suicide bombings and clashes between Israeli troops and Palestinians in the West Bank and Gaza, can be expected to occur. Implementation of the Israeli 'closure' policy[1] will jeopardize the already shaky prospects for the Palestinian economy. Uncertainty will also affect investor confidence in Jordan. For both the Jordanian and Palestinian leaderships, domestic political and economic concerns will loom large. Their ability to coordinate economic policies to mutual benefit will be

---

1 This policy, instituted periodically, involves sealing off the Palestinians in the West Bank and Gaza Strip from access to Israel and East Jerusalem. So-called 'internal closures' involve the sealing off of individual Palestinian cities in the West Bank, preventing Palestinian movement from one to another.

constrained by logistical difficulties. Jordanian–Palestinian relations may suffer as a result. The prospects for stability will be undermined, with potentially grim consequences for all parties.

Contributory and countervailing forces

The situation prevailing in Jordan and in Palestine in late 1997 is not satisfactory to anyone concerned, but an effort of will on the part of the political actors is probably necessary to break out of the general *malaise*. Without the exercise of clear and determined leadership at the top and a seizure of initiative by players at other levels, however, it is easy to envisage a process of *Drift* enduring. The single most important factor contributing to *Drift* is the propensity of both Jordanians and Palestinians to delay taking any decisions about their mutual relations until there is substantive progress on the Israeli–Palestinian track. If that is not forthcoming and the Israelis, whatever their strategic vision, prove unable to seize the initiative either, then *Drift* will result.

There will be contributory and countervailing forces working for and against this scenario coming about at the people-to-people, entity-to-entity and leadership levels, not to mention in the broader regional and international context. The intention here is to explore the most pronounced or potent factors with relevance to this scenario. Some of the issues raised will be pursued further in subsequent chapters. The discussion begins with some thoughts on how the Jordanian and Palestinian leaderships could contribute to *Drift*, notwithstanding their respective visions and aspirations. The focus will then shift to other facets of Jordanian–Palestinian relations which are of equal importance to understanding the whole picture.

Leadership

Neither King Hussein nor President Arafat has shown much inclination to consult closely with each other, coordinate their policies and work towards some form of unity in the future. Both leaders have remained noncommittal on the issue of future ties between Jordan and

Palestine, apparently preferring to await developments on the Israeli–Palestinian track. For its part, the Palestinian leadership may be motivated by a desire to strengthen its position and acquire more sovereign powers and attributes of statehood before entering negotiations with Jordan on formal linkages and cooperation. There is a logic to this position, in that Yasser Arafat and the PLO leadership as a whole would no doubt like to approach such negotiations from a position of greater parity with the Jordanian leadership. For its part, the Jordanian leadership presumably prefers not to prejudge developments, since the fate of the Palestinian entity is so uncertain, and if the circumstances of Palestinians on the West Bank significantly deteriorate elements there might increasingly look to Jordan as a potential protector – especially if the authority of the PA as a whole and of Arafat in particular is progressively eroded.

For both the Jordanian and the Palestinian leaderships, therefore, there is virtue in playing a waiting game, on the issue of Jordanian–Palestinian relations at least. They are thus already contributing to a *Drift* scenario for Jordanian–Palestinian relations and if there is no breakthrough on the Israeli–Palestinian track they could carry on in this vein. In fact, in so far as they hold back from formulating a plan for future Jordanian–Palestinian relations, they forgo one of the options for injecting new life into the Israeli–Palestinian track of negotiations and contribute to *Drift* in the peace process overall. In any case, for present purposes, it is to be assumed that neither King Hussein and his government nor President Arafat and the PLO are able to direct that process onto a more productive footing, even as they continue to talk with the Israelis and others about possible ways forward.

The two leaders may periodically act in unison or parallel, if Israel takes unilateral actions which offend them both. An example of such coordination occurred over the Jerusalem tunnel incident in September 1996. Yet differences between the two leaderships could also prevent Israel from achieving a breakthrough with one at the perceived expense of the other. Arafat and the PLO leadership may be expected to stand in the way of any Israeli moves to increase Jordan's role in the West Bank, for example, though King Hussein himself has been reluctant to go along with any such move in the face of Palestinian resistance.

Political elites

One of the elements which will feature in the calculations of both leaderships is the amount of support they can count on from key sectors in their respective communities. The traditional commercial and rural elite in the West Bank was historically depicted as pro-Jordanian, but since the advent of the PA the younger members of this aristocracy have become more nationalist and forged coalitions with members of the lower-middle-class political elite in Fateh, the predominant faction in the PLO. In Jordan, the conventional wisdom is that nationals of Palestinian origin predominate in the private sector and Tranjordanians enjoy ascendancy in the public sector. While this generalization has some credence, horizontal connections and alliances exist at the most senior levels of both, and key individuals may shift from the private to the public sector and back again with ease. However, in so far as Jordanians of Palestinian origin support the nationalist cause of their brethren across the river, they may be nervous of the consequences for themselves, inside Jordan, if they are seen to be more loyal to Palestine than to the Kingdom.

In both Jordan and the Palestinian entity, elite status derives from service of the state at senior levels, as well as from professional status, social heritage and independent wealth. While there is an overlap between all such sources of power in the community, distinctive groupings are apparent within the elite strata of the two societies.[2] A class of 'state managers' can be found on both sides of the river Jordan, though in the case of Palestine this has come into being only since the advent of the PA. Historically in Jordan and more recently in Palestine, these state managers have a vested interest in enhancing external

---

2 An examination of the distinctive groups within the Jordanian and Palestinian social and economic elites and their links to the political establishment is undertaken in subsequent chapters. The discussion here and in later chapters draws on a working paper prepared by Yezid Sayigh entitled 'Political Elites and the Rentier System'.

sources of support for the state, principally in the form of international aid. This may make for competition rather than cooperation between the state managers or political elites on either side of the river Jordan. They may find themselves competing, for example, for the same pool of resources derived from outside powers such as the United States, Europe and Japan. They may also find it difficult to work in parallel because of the differences between the state systems of Jordan and the Palestinian entity.

The nascent Palestinian system could be characterized as a neo-patrimonial one, using the same distributive practices as those developed and refined by the PLO leadership before the formation of the PA. The PA is the principal provider of new jobs in the Palestinian entity. It also apparently expects to derive income from the approval of contracts for projects to be undertaken in the Palestinian areas or the supply of goods. Pressure to end such practices is unlikely to make headway in the absence of other sources of revenue. Jordan's system runs on a sort of rational bureaucratic model, with a large state bureaucracy and security establishment and a significant role for the state in the economy, in the form of subsidies and protective tariffs. Because of the austerity programme undertaken by Jordan under the auspices of the World Bank and International Monetary Fund (IMF), and the intention to trim down the size of the state, the prospect of 'administrative reform' is viewed with some alarm among East Bankers employed in the state sector. For the business sector, meanwhile, the prospect of liberalization could portend the end of protected status. Sectors of the elite on both sides of the Jordan may be in defensive mood.

Individual members and sectors of the elites in Jordan and Palestine may forge personal ties across the Jordan, or they may shun such links in preference for ties elsewhere – to Israel or Egypt, for example, in the case of Palestinians, and to Syria or Iraq in the case of Jordanians. In this sense they can fuel a trend or help define a pattern of relationships. Also, they may resist acting upon strategic political initiatives undertaken by their respective leaders. An example of such resistance would be the decision of a number of Jordanian professional associations and business interests to hold back on normalization of relations with

Israel. However, for present purposes, it seems entirely plausible that the Jordanian and Palestinian elites will not act in concert to inject new life into the peace process or bilateral Jordanian–Palestinian relations in the absence of a lead from the top.

Instead, it is very likely that these elites could give priority to keeping their status within their own domestic settings and keeping pace with internal political dynamics. Since the establishment of the PA, the political elite in Palestine is predominantly in the PLO (including returnees) and thus mostly based in Gaza. Following Oslo, this elite has capitalized on economic opportunities with Israel and Egypt and is therefore not predisposed to seek out links with Jordan. On the West Bank itself, as mentioned, there has been an evolution in the attitudes of the traditional elite, whose members historically favoured closer ties to Jordan, but who are now jockeying for position under the system established by the PA. Independent businessmen are also pursuing opportunities opened up under the auspices of the PA. On the Jordanian side, in so far as the political elite located in the bureaucracy and security establishment is Transjordanian, it will probably not be enthusiastic about forging closer links to the West Bank. Meanwhile, Jordanian commercial interests see West Bank producers as competitors and a greater opening of the borders would expose Jordan to some cheaper Palestinian products.

In sum, the preoccupations of the political elites will be such that they will probably allow *Drift* to occur, rather than taking any concerted action to halt it. Their role will be more significant under other scenarios, where initiatives will be taken by the political leaders which will require them to react either positively or negatively.

Political parties

The role of the political parties of Jordan and Palestine in any of the scenarios will be more reactive than proactive. This is partly because none of them has devoted any time and effort to developing a position on Jordanian–Palestinian relations, even though most have a stance on the peace process and relations with Israel, and partly because political parties as such have yet to acquire a strong and autonomous role in political life.

In Jordan there are over a dozen legally registered and functioning political parties, established since the passage of the Political Parties Law No. 32 of 1992 enabled them to operate formally. They represent a broad spectrum of political currents and affiliations, some of which date back to the late 1940s and early 1950s, in the period preceding the king's decision in 1957 to ban the political parties of the time and restrict the activities of unions, social and labour organizations. The contemporary parties can be grouped into four broad categories:[3]

(1) The Islamic current includes the Islamic Action Front (the Muslim Brotherhood group) and much smaller Democratic Islamic Arab Movement.

(2) The Arab nationalist current incorporates the Jordanian Socialist Arab Baath Party, which looks to the Iraqi Baath for ideological correctness; the Progressive Arab Baath Party which, by contrast, accords legitimacy to the pan-Arab leadership of the Baath Party in Syria; and the Constitutional Front, which is part of the pan-Arab nationalist current in ideological terms, but has more in common with the centrist trend in terms of its social composition.

(3) The leftist political current includes, on the one hand, the Jordanian Communist Party and its offshoots over time and, on the other hand, parties giving expression to the various factions of the Palestinian nationalist movement and the PLO.

(4) The 'centrist' current embraces those parties which are solidly pro-Hashemite. Within this group is the National Constitutional Party (NCP) headed by Abdul Hadi Al-Majali, which was founded in 1997, bringing together several smaller parties. The hierarchy of this new political force have almost all held senior positions in the Jordanian state and will probably continue to revolve through government. With respect to Jordanian–Palestinian relations, the senior members will likely be able to deliver most of their supporters in accordance with political courses charted by the King.

3 The categorization presented here is based on material in a working paper on the political parties in Jordan prepared by Hani Hourani.

The sheer number of separate parties in Jordan is one explanation for their relative weakness. Also, in contrast to the 1950s to 1970s, when pan-Arab and Palestinian concerns with the question of Palestine were a strong motivator, the parties of the 1990s have to respond more to a plethora of socio-political issues reflective of the complexity of the Jordanian domestic scene. Social life in Jordan is more dependent on geographic origin, religion and age group than on class distinctions, and the electoral law as amended for the 1993 election perpetuated the role of tribal affiliations in Jordanian politics and inhibited the development of modern forms of political mobilization and participation. Also, in the case of Jordan, the character and nature of debate on Jordanian–Palestinian relations reflects the volatility of the issue. It was debated openly only comparatively recently and exploded in 1995 as a result of a survey on Jordanian–Palestinian relations on the Jordanian domestic scene by the Center for Strategic Studies.[4] In early 1997 there was an exchange of views in the press between two senior political figures, Abdul Hadi Al-Majali and Taher Masri. The catalyst for this exchange is also of interest. It stemmed from domestic concerns rather than relations across the river. The impetus came from Trans-jordanian elements, asserting their place in the political spectrum by questioning the loyalty to the state of Jordanians of Palestinian origin, which then brought to the fore the issue of Jordanian–Palestinian relations in general.

In their formal political platforms the Jordanian political parties express no detailed views or preferences for the future of Jordanian–Palestinian relations at the entity-to-entity level, beyond endorsing the establishment of an independent Palestinian state in the West Bank and Gaza. Beyond that, their attitudes can be inferred only from their general ideologies, their constituencies, their relations with the regime (whether pro or anti) and their responses to specific moves by the executive on related issues, such as the terms on which passports are issued to Palestinians.

---

4 Center for Strategic Studies Survey, *Jordanian-Palestinian Relations: Domestic Dimension*, February 1995. Findings of this survey are also discussed in Chapter 5.

Similarly, in Palestine, the political parties have not clearly defined their preferences for the future of Jordanian–Palestinian relations. Also, like their Jordanian counterparts, they are more preoccupied with domestic and immediate concerns than planning for regional relations in the future. Unlike their Jordanian counterparts they are focused on the existential threat presented by the Israeli occupation. The political parties and factions in the Palestinian entity can be grouped into two main trends:

(1) the nationalist trend – which includes Fateh, the Democratic Front for the Liberation of Palestine (DFLP), the Patriotic Front for the Liberation of Palestine (PFLP), Hizb al-Sharb (the People's Party) and Fida (formed by a breakaway faction of the DFLP);
(2) the Islamist trend – including Hamas, Islamic Jihad and the Islamic Liberation Party.

The nationalist trend, with Fateh in the forefront, predominates over the Islamist trend, within which Hamas is predominant. Some new parties have begun to emerge, but have failed to find a foothold.

The performance of the parties in the Palestinian Legislative Council (PLC) elections demonstrated that aside from Fateh and Hamas, the rest virtually do not count. The DFLP and PFLP did not formally run, though two candidates were identified with the DFLP and did not make it into the council. How the outcome would have been different if they had participated officially is not clear. Hizb al-Sharb and Fida ran but gained no seats. Hamas achieved a presence but the composition of the council does not reflect the relative influence of the factions in the society, aside from Fateh. With the exception of Fateh, the various political groupings in the PLC remain weak, fragmented, subject to defections and without strong followings in the community.

None of the main Palestinian factions and parties were founded on the expectation of running for election in the post-Oslo setting. Their ideologies were devised on the basis of the struggle for Palestine with Israel. What now distinguishes them is their position on the peace process, with Hamas officially opposed to anything short of regaining all of Mandatory Palestine, the DFLP and PFLP against Oslo and Fateh in favour of it. Yet all the political factions are as much concerned now about how the PA exercises its authority as they are about dealings with Israel. If present trends continue and Arafat remains at the helm, most foresee an erosion rather than an enhancement of democracy. In the circumstances, therefore, the Palestinian political parties are no better placed than their Jordanian counterparts to drive an agenda for closer Jordanian–Palestinian relations in the absence of an initiative from the president.

In sum, the position and preoccupations of the political parties in Jordan and Palestine are such that they will be more likely to contribute to the realization of the *Drift* scenario than stand in its way.

The media

The Jordanian media have a longer pedigree than their Palestinian counterparts, which are only just taking formal shape. That said, the Jordanian media have not developed an investigative style of journalism in the sense that they could not be characterized as the watch-dog for the public; rather, they seek to reflect trends in society. In this way they provide some clues as to current thinking on key issues, including Jordanian–Palestinian relations. The electronic media are state-controlled and can be characterized as the mouthpiece of government views. The three main Arabic daily newspapers – *Al-Rai*, which has the largest circulation, and *Al Dustour* and *Al-Aswaq*, with minor differences – could be termed establishment papers. None of them has taken the initiative in discussing Jordanian–Palestinian relations, but they have provided the forum for a significant part of the debate in the country. The English-language daily, the *Jordan Times*, has a history of more critical coverage of the news, but its impact on Jordanian society is more limited.

The most pronounced views on all aspects of Jordanian–Palestinian relations, as on other contentious issues, appear in the weekly tabloids, of which there are upwards of twenty in Jordan. Commentators can be quite outspoken in the tabloids, which is what sells them. Aside from the weeklies, which have their own distinct identities, including one Islamist paper, the Jordanian media can be characterized as essentially directionless on the subject of Jordanian–Palestinian relations.

In Palestine the media fall into two categories, the official media, including the very recently established official television channel and Voice of Palestine Radio, and the unofficial media, which aspire to become independent. There are also a number of smaller local television and radio stations, but their interests are purely local. The official television broadcasts are unsophisticated, both in format and content, and news bulletins feature the official engagements of the president more than anything else. The radio is more advanced technically and is popular, but it avoids covering controversial issues. The print media, which are not state-run, are still in the throes of transition from the fighting mode adopted during the Intifada and before. By far the largest-circulation daily is *Al-Quds*, which is also the most objective in its treatment of issues, though the imperative of survival influences its content. Since the establishment of the PA there have been arrests of newspaper editors, and the authorities tried to censor the output of an independent television station dedicated to broadcasting debates in the PLC.

On the whole, Palestinian media toe the official line, either because that is their function or out of self-censorship driven by fear. As a result, coverage of developments in the peace process veers from positive, in accordance with regime policy, to negative in reflection of public disillusionment. Attention to Jordanian–Palestinian relations is minimal, since the subject is peripheral to the preoccupations of both the authorities and the public. However, it is instructive that, owing to the poor quality of the official television service, the Palestinian public prefers to watch either the Israeli Arabic service or Jordanian television. The assessment of specialists who contributed to this study is that, unless and until the media of Jordan and Palestine attain a more independent identity, underpinned by formal protections for press freedom, they will not be able to play a decisive role in mapping the future of Jordanian–Palestinian relations.

Professional associations and other NGOs

Professional associations blossomed in Jordan in the absence of political parties between 1957 and 1989. They established a practice of holding their own elections to office which were relatively free and even if they did not actually criticize the state, they volunteered alternative ways of looking at issues. With the re-emergence of political parties it looked as though such organizations would fall by the wayside; however, they have been galvanized into renewed activity, specifically around the issue of resisting normalization with Israel. Their memberships tend to reflect the relative distribution of East Bankers and Palestinians in the population at large, or certainly in the professions concerned. In this sense they are an antidote to the polarization of society which has become more evident since the establishment of the Palestinian entity across the river.

In Palestine, professional associations and other non-governmental organizations served an important function in the absence of a Palestinian authority, even if some of them became vehicles for the PLO and its various factions, during the years of struggle against Israeli occupation. With the advent of the PA, a number of aid organizations and donor countries have switched their funding to the Authority and away from NGOs. Officials in the PA and Fateh members, meanwhile, have sought to take over the running of the main NGOs. As a consequence, these bodies are in the midst of redefining their role in society and the results are mixed. In so far as prominent figures in Palestinian society speak out against the PA from their platform in NGOs, they can run into trouble with the president, largely because he may interpret an attack on 'the state' as an attack on himself. In Jordan the situation is different, in that criticism of the government is not interpreted as a direct affront to the king.

Broadly speaking, the significance of professional associations and NGOs for Jordanian–Palestinian relations is minimal in Palestine, but of some consequence on the Jordanian domestic front, where membership of the former ignores differences of identity and geographic origin. On another note, however, the NGOs that enjoy royal patronage –

which in turn renders them quasi-governmental organizations – have tended to favour projects benefiting rural, disenfranchised areas, which usually means Transjordanians. This is most apparent in the case of women's organizations. Seeming partiality for a certain constituency need not imply political motivation, however, and could simply be a response to the greatest need.

Public opinion

The above demonstrates that the principal political actors inside both Jordan and Palestine, aside from the political leadership, are reactive and reflective rather than proactive, at least at the strategic level. This suggests that they could easily be swept along in a *Drift* scenario. As will be explored, that scenario could lead to a serious deterioration in living standards on both sides of the river and more fractiousness within both societies. Different groups will respond differently to these developments. Public opinion poll data give some indication of the various popular responses that can be expected.

On the basis of available data in Palestine[5] it emerges that there is strong support in the West Bank and Gaza for economic and political coordination with Jordan, and there has even been considerable support for some form of unity with Jordan, though not at the expense of Palestinian statehood first. Interest in developing connections with Jordan is higher in the West Bank than in Gaza. Age, education and occupation make a difference, with older people more likely than youngsters to support ties to Jordan as opposed to separation. The important point here is that public attitudes towards relations with Jordan are influenced by the performance of the PA, progress or the lack of it in the peace process, and specific actions taken by the Jordanian government. At times when the PA is highly regarded, interest in developing links to Jordan is lower than when it is subject to greater criticism. The more optimistic respondents are about the peace process, the less enthusiasm they show for some form of unity

---

5 In this case derived from surveys conducted by CPRS in January 1994 and October 1995 in particular. More such data will be discussed in Chapter 5.

with Jordan. However, if Jordan is perceived to be standing in the way of Palestinian aspirations to statehood, as for example when the king does something to reinforce his role in protection of the holy sites in Jerusalem, there will be a drop in support for some form of unity. In other words, Palestinians, especially on the West Bank, look to Jordan to help them out when the going gets rough.

Available poll data on attitudes towards Jordanian–Palestinian relations in Jordan[6] have generally focused on issues of polarization and integration within the society. According to what can be gleaned from public opinion surveys, the split between Jordanians and Palestinians in the kingdom since the migrations of the 1990s appears to be around 50/50, if all those with Jordanian passports living on the West Bank are discounted. Palestinians who arrived in Jordan in 1948 see themselves very clearly as Jordanian citizens by now, but they do not see any contradiction between having Jordanian citizenship and more than one identity. Those who have arrived subsequently vary in how they identify themselves. A majority of Palestinians in Jordan support the establishment of a Palestinian state across the river, partly in anticipation of thereafter developing links with the West Bank based on equality. Palestinian refugees in camps in Jordan want their 'right of return' recognized, in anticipation of compensation in lieu of actual return to areas inside Israel. Across the board, Palestinians in Jordan view with nervousness the claims of some East Bankers that they are the only true Jordanians. There is clearly a Transjordanian constituency for the establishment of an independent Palestinian state in the West Bank and Gaza, to reinforce their sense of separate identity. Among the elite in general, and among students (and university professors), the response to suggestions of some form of unity with the West Bank is more likely to be negative than positive. The reverse is true of Palestinian refugees. Under the *Drift* scenario, all the vexed questions will remain open, which will make for neither calm nor open strife, but continued uncertainty.

6 In this case derived from polls conducted by CSS in recent years. A more detailed account appears in Chapter 5.

Economic trends

Prior to the Israeli occupation of the West Bank in 1967 there was a high degree of integration and mutual dependence between the two banks of the Jordan, though some would prefer to characterize the relationship as an internal division of labour. For Palestinian nationalists at the time, the concentration of industry in the East Bank had political connotations and was cause for resentment. Others saw this as the natural outcome of demographic and economic factors. In fact, Palestinian businessmen in Amman, refugees of 1948, were as likely to be the beneficiaries of business contracts and agencies awarded by the government on the East Bank as the Transjordanians were. Then as now, relationships between Palestinian individuals, families and companies straddling the two banks were as instrumental in defining economic relations across the river as macro-economic planning by the Jordanian state.

Following the Israeli occupation of the West Bank, Jordan kept open the bridges and permitted the import of Palestinian products relatively unimpeded. Traffic in the opposite direction was restricted by Israeli regulations on imports to the Occupied Territories. In fact, for nearly two decades the trade flow across the river represented a substantial net gain for the Palestinians, with the value of exports to Jordan exceeding the value of imports by up to $70–80 million per annum by the mid-1980s.[7] Yet, by then, the total value of all trade across the Jordan amounted to only 10 per cent of that between the Palestinians and Israel, with the balance in this case heavily in Israel's favour. The predominant characteristic of this period was the subordination of the Palestinian economy to that of Israel.

Another facet of this period, between 1967 and the mid-1980s, was an increase in the number of Palestinian workers settling in Jordan. During Jordan's boom period in the 1970s, the kingdom had the capacity to import labour. It also served as the bridge between the Occupied Territories and the rest of the Arab world, since Palestinians made their way to jobs in the Gulf region via Jordan. Because of Israel's

---

7 Figures unsourced; provided by a project participant on the basis of personal recollections.

policy of barring the return to the Occupied Territories of those Palestinians who left for jobs elsewhere, the latter often ended up settling in Jordan. Once its own need for imported labour peaked and for fear of an unwanted influx of manpower, in the 1980s the Jordanian government began introducing controls to stem the flow of migration. Some measures were also taken to restrict the import of certain goods, including some agricultural products.

Since the late 1980s, from around the time of Jordan's disengagement from the West Bank and the collapse of the Jordanian dinar, the volume of trade between Jordan and Palestine has dropped off significantly, lifting only marginally after Oslo and the Israel–Jordan agreement. A key reason for this is a decline in the relative competitiveness of Palestinian products, not only in the Jordanian market but also elsewhere in the Arab world. This applies to agricultural produce and other goods. The quality of Palestinian labour has not deteriorated, but production techniques have failed to incorporate new technologies and practices in line with the competition. The Palestinians are not the only ones responsible, however. Progressively, Jordan has set up all kinds of non-tariff and some tariff barriers which affect even competitive Palestinian commodities such as stones and marble. As for agricultural produce, the Palestinians cannot hope to compete with the prices of home-grown products in Jordan, because Jordanian agriculture benefits from an array of direct and indirect subsidies. Despite these explanations connected with product quality and prices, the factors impeding Jordanian–Palestinian trade also derive from political circumstances and sensitivities.

As will be seen in Chapters 4 and 5, there are rational, practical reasons for increased Jordanian–Palestinian cooperation in the economic sphere, and there are serious obstacles to closer integration, not least the fact that the two economies are competitors in many sectors. To overcome the obstacles and apply the logic of increased cooperation will require the political will which, as discussed above, may be lacking. The *Drift* scenario implies that the impediments will not be removed and incompatibilities will persist, with marginal gains for some businesses, but no overall restructuring.

On the question of *water* the status quo will endure unless there is movement on the Israeli–Palestinian track, because of the way in which the agreements reached thus far have dealt with the problem. The Palestinians are holding out for a share of the Jordan Basin resources, also drawn on by Israel and Jordan, on the basis of the Johnston Plan of the 1950s which assumed that the West Bank would be accommodated within the total apportioned to Jordan. The deal worked out between Jordan and Israel at Wadi Arabah in August 1995 does not provide for the West Bank, on the assumption that the Palestinians must eventually obtain a share of Yarmouk river water at the expense of Syria, which has taken more than it was originally allocated by Johnston. Meanwhile, since the Johnston Plan was devised, the size of the population on the East Bank has overtaken that on the West Bank. This implies that Jordan is entitled to a greater share relative to the West Bank than originally envisaged, but the matter cannot ultimately be settled without the involvement of Israel.

The Israeli government

By definition, the *Drift* scenario assumes that the Israeli government will prove as powerless as the Palestinians and Jordanians to effect a strategy to break out of the general malaise. It is not difficult to identify factors which could prevent the Israeli government from pushing forward with a strategic plan of its own. Political crises have beset Prime Minister Netanyahu's government since it came to power. Ministers have either resigned or threatened to do so, and Netanyahu has had to concede to the preferences and policy platforms of his various coalition partners in order to keep the coalition together. Within his cabinet he has Likud hardliners such as Ariel Sharon and conservatives in the religious parties with their own agendas. The hardliners, if not the religious party members, would threaten to abandon Netanyahu if he opted for a territorial compromise with the Palestinians that gave them a toe-hold in Jerusalem, abandoned Jewish settlements or sacrificed perceived security needs such as a military presence in the Jordan Valley and access roads to settlements. The most he can propose openly in the way of a formula is his so-called 'Allon-Plus' plan, which, as discussed in Chapter 1, the Palestinians cannot accept.

Drift could therefore prevail if the Israeli government remains of the same basic composition as in mid-1997. In any case, Israeli public opinion is divided on how to proceed with the Palestinians. On the one hand are those in favour of conceding more in order to give the Palestinians an incentive to cooperate. On the other hand, there are those who argue against conceding any more unless and until the Palestinian side delivers better security for Israelis. Under the leadership of Netanyahu, or someone similar, the prime minister can propose and the Palestinians will oppose, and vice versa. If what is on offer from Israel is rejected out of hand by the Palestinians, the Jordanian leadership will not openly endorse what Arafat and the PLO leadership cannot accept.

The international community

Meanwhile, the international community could prove powerless to break the impasse, except in small steps such as rejuvenating peace talks, which could easily be derailed again as they were by the Palestinian suicide bombings in Jerusalem in July and September 1997.

As on these occasions, Israeli *security measures* could be implemented to close off the West Bank and Gaza Strip, surround the main Palestinian towns inside the West Bank with Israeli troops, cut off tax returns to the PA from Israel and generally institute a state of emergency. It would be possible in these circumstances that fear of the consequences of a prolonged crisis would galvanize all the players, including the United States and others, into renewed efforts to restore Israel–Palestinian dialogue. This would be the stop-go pattern of the *Drift* scenario in action.

Implications

If none of the principal parties to the peace process is driving developments, it can be assumed that each of the leaderships will nonetheless be preoccupied with responding to pressures from their various constituencies. For Yasser Arafat and his leadership the priorities will be to consolidate control over Palestinian territory and people, improve security, fight corruption and relieve economic hardship, including obtaining a continuous flow of cash to pay salaries and cement support within the community. If lack of business development prevents the indigenous generation of wealth, and sporadic implementation of the closure policy by Israel prevents more than a few thousand Palestinians from working consistently in Israel, the economic circumstances of the Palestinian population will worsen. Arafat will therefore have to look to the donor countries to keep paying the PA's running costs and will presumably blame lack of progress in the peace process and Israeli closure policies for his predicament.

Drift is a description of the continuation of developments on the ground since mid-1996. Israeli redeployments from Gaza and in the West Bank have signified progress on the one hand, but a new level of Israeli security control and worsening economic conditions inside the Palestinian areas on the other. In a report published by the IMF in March 1997 it was pointed out that Palestinian unemployment nearly doubled and per capita income fell by one-fifth between the signing of Oslo I in 1993 and the end of 1996.[8] Unemployment stood at 34.2 per cent and per capita GNP at around $1,200 in the West Bank and $700 in Gaza at the end of 1996. In other words, the Palestinian leadership will be unable to deliver a peace dividend, but with donor money and Palestinian tax returns transferred from Israel it could still keep paying the salaries of bureaucrats and the police. The Palestinian public may be expected to blame Israel rather than their own leadership for the hardships, and thus the PA could retain control.

However, President Arafat's position is not necessarily secure under the *Drift* scenario. In July 1997 the PLC issued a report by a panel of its members revealing widespread corruption and mismanagement of

---

8 *Recent Economic Developments, Prospects and Progress in Institution Building in the West Bank and Gaza Strip*, report by the Middle Eastern Department, International Monetary Fund, Washington, March 1997; see David Gardner, 'Gloom over Palestinian economy', *Financial Times*, 7 March 1997.

public funds by the PA. On the basis of this the 88-member council voted 56–4 in favour of a resolution calling on the president to dissolve his cabinet and appoint a more competent and professional team in its stead. All but two of the 18-member cabinet tendered their resignations as a result, but Arafat indicated that the time was not right to reach a decision on such matters, given the state of emergency in relations with the Israelis following the suicide bombings at the Mahane Yehuda marketplace in West Jerusalem. These developments serve to demonstrate Arafat's vulnerability and a progressive erosion of support for the PA.

In the teeth of this crisis Arafat made one of his exceptional trips to Jordan to consult King Hussein. The lesson in this is the capacity of the Palestinian leadership to turn to Jordan for help *in extremis*. This reflects a parallel attitude among the Palestinian public in the West Bank, who, according to the opinion polls discussed above, tend to look to Jordan for assistance when the PA is in greatest disrepute and the going gets tough with the Israelis. Under the *Drift* scenario there are likely to be more instances of this kind. The results will depend on how the Jordanian leadership plays its hand. Any moves made by the king which appear to circumvent Arafat in dealings with the Israelis and pose a 'Jordanian option' in place of Palestinian independence, on the West Bank at least, would rekindle Palestinian suspicions there. That said, if Arafat fails utterly to appease his critics within the Palestinian community on issues such as clean government, democracy and human rights, and engages in activities designed first and foremost to meet Israeli demands for a comprehensive crackdown on Islamist and other elements deemed capable of attacking Israelis, there may be those in the West Bank who see some sort of 'Jordanian option' as worth consideration.

Such a development would produce a backlash in Jordan, however. East Bankers nervous of an extension of Jordan's role in the West Bank would not remain quiescent. Palestinians in Jordan would be caught between hostility from Transjordanian nationalists within and concern for the fate of their kin on the West Bank. In the circumstances, King Hussein may well choose not to entertain a 'Jordanian option', and seek instead to push for a resumption of progress on the

Israeli–Palestinian negotiating track. His success in this will depend on help from other sources. The worse the incidence of violence and the greater the chances of escalation, the more likely it will be that the United States intervenes to re-engage the parties at the negotiating table. Under the *Drift* scenario, therefore, the peace process need not collapse totally, but might limp along from crisis to crisis, taking a further toll on confidence in the Palestinian economy.

For Jordan the implications of *Drift* need not be critical in the near term, but will impede economic growth because of the effects on investor confidence. Jordan has implemented some structural changes and policy shifts urged upon it by the World Bank and IMF to attract more inward investment. The problem is that it is a tiny market by itself and can only attract big development and industrial schemes if it represents the gateway to a wider region. Popular will could very well resist economic integration with Israel, and possibly thereby Palestine, in the face of Palestinian difficulties in the peace process. Since the advent of Netanyahu in Israel, public opinion in Jordan has hardened against normalization with the Jewish state. Meanwhile, as discussed previously, there are some socio-political impediments to bolstering business activities in the kingdom in a way that seemingly benefits citizens of Palestinian origin in the business community more than East Bankers in the bureaucracy.

The wild card for Jordan in terms of the *Drift* scenario is future developments in Iraq. Were that country to be allowed to resume normal trade relations, Jordanians would readily turn their sights eastwards to redevelop economic links. Such an eventuality would give the Jordanian economy a breathing space, but would not produce the important and far-reaching benefits of a fundamental shift towards peaceful and profitable economic relations between Israel, Jordan and Palestine. In any case, for present purposes, it may be assumed that Iraq's rehabilitation is still a long way off. Consequently, the Jordanian economy is trapped within the politics of the Jordan-Palestine-Israel triangle and will be unable to flourish under the *Drift* scenario.

Declining living standards need not spell instant eruptions into street riots in Jordan, but the precedents are there. Removal of bread subsidies in 1996 produced protests in Karak. There is also the potential for unrest at the inter-community level, as illustrated when crowds clashed at a football match in Amman in 1996.[9] Some East Banker nationalists are capable of blaming the Palestinians in their midst for a variety of ills and, as mentioned, they fear that the king might be drawn into closer engagement with Palestinian concerns on the West Bank. On both the political and the economic front, therefore, King Hussein's room for manoeuvre will be constrained if *Drift* sets in and he will have to continue his traditional delicate balancing act, both at the domestic and at the regional level.

Assuming two or three years of *Drift*, with the peace process suffering but surviving and the three leaders, King Hussein, President Arafat and Prime Minister Netanyahu all in place and concentrating on their domestic constituencies, the consequence for Jordanian–Palestinian relations will be fractiousness. Violence will recur on the Israeli–Palestinian front. Arafat may periodically seek King Hussein's assistance. The latter could be instrumental in preventing implementation of some Israeli decisions, for example on an issue affecting the Muslim holy sites in Jerusalem. Arafat could benefit, but if he felt sidelined he could take this as Jordanian meddling. Mutual suspicion would therefore flourish, not diminish, between the leaderships.

In formulating its own legal and institutional arrangements for Palestine the PA could take a number of steps designed to snub Jordan and part company with Jordanian law and practices, but on a piecemeal, not strategically planned or coordinated, basis. The prospects for bilateral economic relations would suffer accordingly and in the name of political solidarity, at the popular level, little would be done to surmount the obstacles to greater economic interchange.

Outcomes

At the end of the two- to three-year period of *Drift*, if the peace process

---

9 Perhaps it is worth mentioning here, to keep a sense of proportion, that Palestinians and East Bankers all celebrated in unison when the Jordanian football team won at the Arab Games in Beirut in 1997.

is still alive, the Jordanian and Palestinian economies will be in a worse state than at the beginning of 1997. Their respective political systems will not manifest greater openness or wider participation in decision-making. There will be more discontinuities and incompatibilities between their legal and educational systems. Contacts between members of the two communities across the river will be the object of suspicion, either by the authorities, or by other elements in the two communities. Cooperation between the Jordanian and Palestinian leaderships will be sporadic and limited to moments of crisis in the peace process. Both entities will be weaker in relation to Israel.

This outcome assumes that the peace process does not totally collapse, and logically it would be accompanied by *Drift* on the Israeli–Palestinian track, as outlined in Chapter 1. Alternatively, it could involve a *de facto* version of *Autonomy-Plus* on the Israeli–Palestinian dimension of trilateral relations, as also defined in Chapter 1. This possibility receives greater attention in Chapter 3. If, however, there is *Breakdown* in Israeli–Palestinian relations and the peace process disintegrates into renewed confrontation and a reversal of the Oslo process on that front, the consequences will be very serious for all parties. In contrast to the situation before Oslo, the Palestinians now possess an armed police force. Israeli tanks and artillery could overpower Palestinian firepower, but at tremendous cost in lives on both sides. Jordan would presumably seek to insulate itself from an overflow of violence from the West Bank. That would mean tighter security arrangements along the Jordan and a policy of containment. If a new wave of Palestinian refugees looked likely, the Jordanian leadership would face difficulties if they were refused refuge or if they were allowed to enter Jordan and put domestic security at risk. In this sense, *Drift* in Jordanian–Palestinian relations could leave both parties very ill-prepared for the consequences of renewed Israeli–Palestinian conflict.

A note on Jerusalem

With respect to Jerusalem in particular, under the *Drift* scenario King Hussein would be likely to retain his role as custodian of the Muslim holy sites. No new institutional arrangements for custodianship of the Christian holy sites would be made – the Arab Church would consider Jordan as its address and various international Christian bodies would periodically voice their concerns about access under Israeli control. Israel would retain *de facto* sovereignty while the Palestinians would continue asserting their claims to sovereignty. In the event that Palestinian elections could still be held, those living in Jerusalem would presumably exercise circumscribed rights to vote. They would, no doubt, still be able to hold Jordanian passports, but without rights of citizenship or extended residency in Jordan and they would also carry Israeli travel documents denoting their residence in the city. That said, the Israeli authorities could be expected to persist in their efforts to remove Jerusalem residency from as many Palestinians as possible.

3 THE *FUNCTIONAL* SCENARIO

Here the term *Functional* refers to the powers accruing to the Palestinians within autonomous areas in the West Bank and Gaza and a three-way division of labour between Israel, Jordan and the Palestinians. The question of sovereignty in the West Bank would be left indeterminate. In other words, this scenario describes what could happen if the Palestinians achieve no more than functional autonomy in the West Bank and Gaza. The premise for this scenario, and what distinguishes it from *Drift*, is that a hardline Israeli leadership takes the driving seat, while the Palestinian and Jordanian leaderships are in reactive mode, responding to incidents and developments, but unable to grasp the initiative to direct events.

It may be assumed that the Palestinians will not agree to functional autonomy as an acceptable final and formal outcome of their entry into the peace process and on-going dealings with the Israelis. It could be what they end up with, however, if negotiations fail to yield an alternative they can accept, and neither they, nor the Jordanians, nor any external actors do anything to redirect the dynamic at work. Under this scenario, therefore, the dominant force is a government in Israel with an agenda to resist the emergence of an independent Palestinian state, yet willing to accept functional autonomy in circumscribed areas. The outcome would be likely to place a continuing burden on Jordan to help the Palestinians deal with the consequences. To draw him in, conceivably, King Hussein could be offered inducements, in the form of promises by Israel that it would concede more to him on the West Bank, including more territory, than it would to a Palestinian leadership. The intention would be to persuade the king that he can deliver more to the Palestinians than the PLO.

The *Functional* scenario would presumably mean something very different from the *Separation* scenario (discussed in the next chapter), in so far as Palestinians would look to Jordan for the provision of passports and various forms of cooperation in the political and economic spheres. The situation would differ fundamentally from the *Cooperation* scenario (explored in Chapter 5), however, because the Palestinians and Jordanians would not have decided to cooperate as a strategic choice and would not have set about it in a systematic manner.

Contributory and countervailing forces

In this scenario the nature, agenda and determination of the Israeli government will be of central importance. Israel must be able and willing to manage events according to its own agenda and the Jordanians and Palestinians must permit this to occur, whether willingly or not. Israel's objective must be *Autonomy-Plus* for the Palestinians on the West Bank, as defined in Chapter 1. It may be assumed, therefore, that the Israeli government is of a centre-right complexion and the Likud-led coalition headed by Prime Minister Netanyahu could qualify.

Autonomy-Plus, by definition, is a mechanism for preventing Palestinian statehood. As outlined in Chapter 1, the main features of *Autonomy-Plus* are as follows:

- functional autonomy for the Palestinians over their civil affairs and internal security;
- no Palestinian army or heavy armour;
- maintenance of Israeli control over water;
- maintenance of the Israeli military presence in the Jordan Valley;
- maintenance of Israeli military surveillance arrangements on high ground;
- Israeli control of the air space;
- maintenance of Israeli settlements directly under Israeli sovereignty;
- maintenance of Israeli control of communication links.

Supporters of this formula can be found on the Israeli right, in the settler community and among the religious nationalists and Orthodox community. Its appeal to secularists on the right of the Israeli political spectrum lies in its provisions for Israeli security. Though some security specialists have come to question the value of maintaining an Israeli military presence in the Jordan Valley, partly on the grounds that Israel has now signed a peace treaty with Jordan, which gives it a new security buffer to the east, the conventional wisdom in Israel has been that the whole West Bank is a security buffer against threats from the east and that Israel must therefore have a forward presence on the front line. *Autonomy-Plus* also provides for Israel to retain overall control of strategic assets in the West Bank, including all border crossings to Jordan, the high ground, all the air space and water resources. Under *Autonomy-Plus* Israeli access to anywhere in the West Bank would be unimpeded, except that Palestinian police and others could be expected to put up resistance to a re-entry into the main Palestinian towns (Area A under the Oslo formula). Link routes from west to east and to all the settlements would not have to be negotiated with the Palestinians, as under the *Fifty-Fifty Solution*, for example, since the issue would not be up for discussion.

In contrast to the period preceding Oslo, however, Israel would not have to bear the chore, so to speak, of managing Palestinian civil administration. Civil policing duties and internal security in Palestinian population centres could also be a Palestinian responsibility under *Autonomy-Plus*, but the Palestinian police would not be allowed to obtain armour and the Israelis would still have the facility to control security outside and around all the main Palestinian towns, enabling them to impose the kinds of internal closures on those towns that were implemented in the wake of the Jerusalem bombings in July and September 1997. Above all, by preventing the emergence of a Palestinian state, hardline Israelis could rest assured that they had not facilitated the creation of a new Arab state on their very doorstep which, according to the foreboding of some rightwingers, could obtain arms and one day wage some sort of war on Israel proper.

Jewish settlers would be able to remain in place under Israeli control, with maximum military protection from would-be attackers. Religious nationalists and 'Greater Israel' ideologues would have to make no formal compromises on sovereignty over the West Bank and its Jewish holy sites. Jerusalem would be undivided under *de facto* Israeli sovereignty. For the religious Orthodox, meanwhile, *Autonomy-Plus* and thence the *Functional* scenario would bring the advantage of not having to face decisions about whether or not it is permissible to compromise on such issues.

Political dynamics in Israel

On the basis of the foregoing description, an Israeli government could certainly identify a constituency for *Autonomy-Plus* and the *Functional* scenario, and there are facets of that constituency in Netanyahu's Likudnik coalition. That said, this formula would have its opponents. The small Arab contingent in the Knesset, Meretz and the left and centre of the Labour Party believe in the merits of Palestinian statehood, or something approaching it, in the West Bank and Gaza, on political, ideological and security grounds. Israeli Arabs have embraced the aspiration of Palestinian statehood, even if they would not choose to change their own citizenship. Meretz members talk of the immorality of occupation of another people. Labour supporters of Palestinian statehood emphasize the virtues of separation from the Palestinians in the name of preserving Israeli democracy and its Jewish character. More broadly, there is a body of opinion in Israel which believes a two-state solution is needed on security grounds. According to this view, *Autonomy-Plus* will not work because the Palestinians will not agree to it and therefore the struggle will continue, spelling ever more violence and loss of life for Israeli civilians and soldiers alike.

The existence of this body of opinion will place the onus on an Israeli government committed to *Autonomy-Plus* to defy its critics and succeed in pushing through its agenda despite them. It seems likely, therefore, that such a government will choose to pursue its objectives by stealth rather than consensus, at least until it has achieved some results. In other words, the strategy would be to create more and more 'facts on the ground' that reinforce an *Autonomy-Plus* outcome, and to avoid putting this strategy to a vote in the Knesset. This would mean stalling progress on the implementation of Oslo and forestalling progress on final status talks with the Palestinians by offering only unacceptable negotiating gambits, while reinforcing settlements and expanding the road network linking up Israeli assets in the West Bank. The question then becomes, what will the Palestinians and Jordanians, among others, do to impede or facilitate such an Israeli strategy?

The Palestinian leadership

Yasser Arafat and the PLO could never agree to *Autonomy-Plus* since their whole objective is independent Palestinian statehood in the West Bank and Gaza with a capital in Jerusalem. Furthermore, Arafat has staked his reputation on his capacity to achieve this. It was he who opted for the Oslo formula instead of the more ambitious line being pursued by the official Palestinian negotiating team in the Washington peace talks in 1992–93. He appeared to be vindicated when Israel's Labour government implemented the first redeployments out of Gaza and Palestinian population centres in the West Bank under the Oslo process. The Palestinian leadership was duly mortified when Labour lost the 1996 election and they found themselves dealing with an Israeli government profoundly critical of the Oslo formula and a prime minister reluctant even to meet the Palestinian president.

At that time Arafat and his advisers discussed how to respond to the negative turn of events. A very few argued that a Likud-led government could deliver a deal more effectively than its Labour counterpart, basing their argument on the precedent of Menachem Begin's peace agreement with Egypt. The majority view in the Palestinian leadership was less sanguine. Some advised hunkering down and waiting out the duration of the Netanyahu government, using the time to consolidate in Gaza and pursue objectives such as an airport and seaport in the Strip, which the Israelis were thought potentially ready to concede as a sop for lack of progress on the West Bank. Meanwhile, the Palestinians could make greater efforts to reach out to the Israeli public and bolster the position of the peace camp. The US State Department and some members of the American Jewish community were also identified as potential allies in bringing the Israeli leadership round to a more accommodating position. In addition, with the help of Syria and Egypt, the Palestinian leadership could renew calls for Arab solidarity and try to dissuade other Arab states from going ahead with normalizing relations with Israel.

Faced with an Israeli government apparently dedicated to implementing no more than *Autonomy-Plus* on the West Bank if not in Gaza, the Palestinian leader could be expected to proceed in this general manner. However, his position could be seriously weakened over time, which would strengthen the ability of the Israeli government to push through its agenda. Arafat's style of leadership has been to reward key groups of supporters within the Palestinian community without due regard for the fallout. The acquisition of personal fortunes by officials in his administration and their conspicuous spending in a time of increasing hardship for ordinary Palestinians has fuelled resentment and criticism, as illustrated in the report on corruption and incompetence in the cabinet issued by the PLC in July 1997 and the council's call for resignations.[1]

Meanwhile, by resorting to various measures to pressurize the Israeli government, Arafat could end up merely reinforcing Israeli suspicions. He did indeed run into difficulties with the United States and some of his potential apologists in Israel by turning on and off security cooperation between the Palestinian police and the Israeli security forces between June 1996 and August 1997. This bolstered the Israeli government's case for saying that he had not made enough effort to rein in extremists on the Palestinian side. When, immediately after his election, Netanyahu initially refused to deal directly with the Palestinian leadership, the latter reduced all security cooperation with the Israelis to just one channel. Thereafter, the level of cooperation was expanded and contracted in accordance with developments. To protest against Netanyahu's decision to go ahead with the Har Homa settlement at Jebel Abu Ghneim, for example, cooperation was almost ended. However, the ploy backfired when suicide bombers struck in

---

1 'Arafat given one month to replace cabinet', *Jerusalem Post*, 1 August 1997.

Jerusalem and Arafat was accused by Netanyahu of not doing enough to contain the threat of terror. That left the Palestinian leader under severe pressure from Israel and the United States to do more to restrain extremists, including, at one stage, an Israeli call for the arrest of the Palestinian police chief, before Israel would agree to any resumption of peace talks.[2] Israel also stopped payment of Palestinian tax returns to the PA, which at the time accounted for about two-thirds of the PA's annual revenue,[3] thereby undercutting its ability to pay official and police salaries.

These developments demonstrate the way in which Arafat and his leadership could find their authority weakened under the *Functional* scenario. If their strategy merely ended up bolstering the case of hardliners in Israel while losing Arafat the ability to reward supporters within his own community, it could also presage a shift in Jordan's position.

The Jordanian leadership

King Hussein of Jordan could not formally endorse an Israeli strategy for *Autonomy-Plus*, but he could find himself drawn in to the Israeli agenda. This could come about if Israeli manoeuvres and the reactions of Arafat and the PLO progressively weakened the authority of the PA, thereby opening up a vacuum which Jordan would end up filling for fear of something worse. The scenario depicted here is called the *Functional* scenario because it posits a sharing of functional responsibilities in the West Bank not only between Israel and the Palestinians, if all that the latter obtain from the Israelis is *Autonomy-Plus*, but also involving Jordan.

As discussed in Chapter 1, in the Israel-Palestine-Jordan triangle, no single one of the players can stand entirely alone; all are bound in to one strategic space by Palestinians in all three communities and a measure of economic interdependence. Jordan continues to provide passports for West Bank Palestinians, albeit on different terms from

---

2 Jay Bushinsky, 'PM: Arafat has done "damn all"', *Jerusalem Post,* 1 August 1997; Douglas Jehl, 'U.S. Is to Referee Suicide Bomb Feud', *International Herald Tribune,* 13 August 1997.

3 Douglas Jehl, 'A Squeeze on Palestinian Budget', *International Herald Tribune,* 6 August 1997.

those issued to citizens in Jordan, and if no other passports were forthcoming, it would have to continue the arrangement.[4] The Jordanian dinar is used on the West Bank, along with the Israeli shekel. Under the *Functional* scenario, this arrangement would presumably continue, thereby enmeshing Jordan in the economic fortunes of the West Bank. For Jordan's role actually to increase would require Arafat's position to continue to erode and the emergence of voices in support of greater Jordanian involvement, which could begin to influence the king's assessment of the situation. Encouragement could come from West Bankers, from the Israelis and from the United States.

When the Oslo process appeared to be making progress, admittedly with periodic setbacks, in 1995–96, King Hussein made a number of statements to the effect that Jordan was not interested in regaining responsibility on the West Bank. He noted, for example, that since he had turned down a suggestion from Israel years before that 98 per cent of the West Bank revert from Israeli occupation to Jordanian rule, he was hardly likely to be interested in competing for something significantly less than that. Following Netanyahu's victory, Jordan went along with the calls for renewed Arab solidarity and a slowdown in the normalization process with Israel, which were voiced by Arab leaders at a mini-summit in Cairo in June 1996.

However, King Hussein could be pressed to reconsider the Jordanian position. The impetus could come from both Israel and the United States, with which the king has enjoyed increasing favour since the end of the Gulf war and Jordan's commitment to peace with Israel. Whereas Arafat is disliked if not distrusted or hated in Israel, King Hussein enjoys enormous popularity with the Israeli public. An Israeli government seeking to prevent the emergence of a Palestinian state, at least on the West Bank, could plausibly identify him as a partner in the endeavour. The facts of Jordan's historical relations with the Palestinians might provide the Israelis with an opening.

---

4 In October 1997, in response to a case brought before the Jordanian Supreme Court by a West Bank Palestinian, the judges ruled that the man could not be denied a five-year Jordanian passport, reaffirming that the 1988 'disengagement' from the West Bank has not been recognized in Jordanian law.

Ever since the establishment of the Jordanian state in 1921 it has been intimately involved in Palestinian affairs. In 1950 the geographic state was extended to include the West Bank, including Arab East Jerusalem – Israel having been established in the rest of Mandatory Palestine apart from the Gaza Strip. The West Bank was of course lost to Israel in the war of 1967 and Jordan has called ever since for its liberation. If the Palestinian leadership, which seemed to stand a chance of furthering this goal under the Oslo process, were to be denied the power to deliver, Jordan could then come under pressure to step in instead, if only on the grounds that otherwise all would be lost.

An Israeli government could try to argue that Arafat lacked either the will or the capacity to control violent and extremist elements in Palestine and that the emergence of a Palestinian state between Israel and Jordan dominated by such forces would be a danger to them both. Israel could also try to recruit Jordan into participating in a security regime in the Jordan Valley to contain the Palestinians and to protect Jordan itself from them and bolster its position in relation to other powers such as Iraq and Syria. The United States could add its voice to this perspective, having identified Jordan as a sympathetic and reliable ally in a dangerous neighbourhood. Economic inducements could be added to security guarantees.

All such approaches would probably fail to sway the king unless they were accompanied by the emergence of a significant Palestinian constituency for increased Jordanian involvement in the West Bank.

Mutual suspicions

Jordanian–Palestinian relations are, as described in Chapter 1, suffused with mutual suspicions. Palestinian nationalists in the West Bank and Gaza have long harboured the fear that the Jordanian government has plotted behind the scenes with the Israelis to prevent an independent Palestinian state emerging on the West Bank. In early 1996, in the run-up to the Israeli elections and after the Palestinian suicide bombings had blighted the electoral chances of Shimon Peres, there were some Palestinians close to Arafat who were telling him that King Hussein wanted a Netanyahu victory, was aware of Hamas activities and was doing nothing to prevent them from the Jordanian side. These same advisers argued that King Hussein would receive favourably a Likud approach for a 'Jordanian option' on the West Bank. Then, when Netanyahu came to power there was a sense of a prophecy come true and near panic among some officials in the PA. Some thought that, even if unwillingly, the king could be forced into complicity by the Israelis and the United States.

Other voices on the Palestinian side cautioned against such alarmist readings of the situation and promoted the idea of reaching a formal understanding with King Hussein to head off any dangers. Nonetheless, some of the worries of the Palestinian leadership about Jordanian subterfuge found their way to the street. The public noted that Jordan's official response to the Israeli election result was perhaps the most relaxed of any Arab government. There were instances in connection with Jerusalem when suspicions were raised about the king's intentions. However, a number of his statements and gestures belied such concerns. In October 1996 he made a show of support for Arafat by accompanying him on a visit to Jericho. On various occasions he has given vent publicly to impatience with Netanyahu, to the point where he wrote the Israeli prime minister a stinging letter of criticism in March 1997.[5]

There are two key factors to take into account here. One is the fact that certain actions or statements by the king fuel Palestinian suspicions if they appear to smack of collusion with the Israelis at Palestinian expense. The other is the relative standing and popularity of Arafat and the PA. As noted in previous chapters, Palestinian public opinion is better disposed towards King Hussein when the reputation of Arafat and the PA is at a low ebb, the peace process appears to be going nowhere and the king himself refrains from actions which appear deliberately to undercut the PA. Consequently, if Arafat's authority is

---

5 As it happens, one commentator in the Israeli press claimed at the time that King Hussein was furious with Netanyahu because he had gone back on a promise to involve Jordan more in the peace process at the expense of the Palestinians. See Yigal Karmon, 'The Real Reasons for King Hussein's Anger', *Yediot Ahronot*, 12 March 1997.

so weakened that the Palestinians themselves look to the king for help, the *Functional* scenario becomes that much more plausible.

Palestinian political elites, factions and parties

Under the *Functional* scenario the Israeli government would not hand over additional land to the Palestinian Authority; it would simply allow Palestinians to continue handling their own civilian and internal security concerns, the latter within limits. Consequently, there would not be a roll-back of the Israeli presence in the West Bank and Gaza and it would not be possible for the Palestinians to link up the areas of their greatest population density into a single land mass in the West Bank. Physical communication between the two would remain difficult and unpredictable. The result could be a fragmentation of authority, with a growing divide between Gaza and the West Bank, the isolation of East Jerusalem from both, and even interchange between the towns of the West Bank impeded. Presumably Arafat and the PA would be in a position to consolidate in Gaza, but the PLC would probably be out on a limb in Ramallah. The municipal councils of the West Bank towns would shoulder most of the responsibility for civil affairs without effective coordination. The Palestinian security apparatus, headquartered in Jericho, would have to operate in disconnected pockets.

Individuals living in the West Bank would presumably be able to make visits to Jordan, which could facilitate their forming closer links with business and family connections there. There could be a re-emergence of elements of the old, pro-Jordanian Palestinian elite as a stronger voice on the West Bank, capable of making direct contacts with King Hussein to keep him apprised of their concerns, if no more than that. However, the West Bank community could also witness the rise of a more independent stream in Fateh with representation in the PLC, the security forces and the municipal councils, which could be something of a power unto itself and not always amenable to Arafat's leadership. Disillusionment with the peace process does not necessarily translate into growing support for Hamas at the expense of the secularist mainstream. Admittedly, Hamas has always been critical of the peace process and it has always operated at the grass-roots level through the mosques and welfare organizations. This would imply that disenchantment with the peace process and frustration with corruption in the PA would naturally lead to a swelling of the ranks of the Islamist movements. Yet if a new, young and determined leadership takes shape within Fateh, it could pose a significant challenge to the PA alongside Hamas activists, at least in the West Bank. Relations with Jordan would then depend on how much Jordan could help West Bank Palestinians cope with and even overcome economic hardships.

In the Gaza Strip the Palestinian president could try to coopt Hamas within the ranks of the Palestinian authority. Arafat could preside over this as a strategy for preventing Hamas from reasserting itself at his expense in conjunction with sister movements in Jordan and Lebanon.

Such developments would actually reinforce realization of the *Functional* scenario in certain respects. The fragmentation of the Palestinian administrative apparatus would underline the reality of *Autonomy-Plus* rather than Palestinian statehood. Meanwhile, in so far as Hamas became more integrated with the PA, at least in Gaza, and a more hardline strain of Fateh began to take shape in the West Bank, such phenomena would confirm Israeli fears that the Palestinian authorities could be incubating something much more hostile to Israel than was envisaged at the time of the Oslo accords. It would be a logical response to resist the formation of a Palestinian state on the one hand and to try to bolster links between Jordan and sympathetic elements in the West Bank, as an antidote to Hamas and hardline nationalists, on the other.

However, between them an Israeli government, a pro-Jordanian faction in the West Bank and a presumably ambivalent King Hussein could not expect to render *Autonomy-Plus* palatable to the bulk of the Palestinian community without devising some demonstrable benefits. Meanwhile, a segment of East Bank Jordanians would probably become agitated at the implications.

Jordanian political elites, factions and parties

For East Bank nationalists the so-called 'Jordanian option' represents a Trojan Horse for Palestinian ascendancy at the expense of Transjordanian identity. In the short term, their fear would focus on the issue of passports. The more Palestinians were granted full passports, the greater the dilution of the Transjordanian position. In the longer term, there would be concern about the influence of West Bank politics on decision-making in Jordan. The more the Jordanian government was drawn in to a *Functional* scenario, the more it would have to take into account the needs of West Bankers as well as Jordanians. East Bank nationalists do not want to share a state with a majority of Palestinians and they have been asserting Jordanian nationalism in juxtaposition to Palestinian nationalism.

The 1988 disengagement from the West Bank removed the constitutional obstacle to holding elections in Jordan. The 1989 riots in the south of the country then gave impetus to the initiation of the process towards political liberalization. Against this backdrop, East Bank nationalists represented in the 'centrist' trend in Jordanian politics want to concentrate on developing agendas for Jordan, not Palestine. Those who identify with the Arab nationalist current would not embrace the *Functional* scenario either. To the extent that Jordan could end up facilitating realization of an Israeli scheme to deny the Palestinians independent statehood, Jordanians identifying themselves with the cause of Arab nationalism, whether of a Syrian, Iraqi or other persuasion, would find themselves party to a betrayal of that cause. Within this range of political forces opposed to the *Functional* scenario the small but vocal segment of hardline or radical East Bank nationalists would also feature.

Security

Such elements in Jordan could be expected to speak out vociferously against a 'Jordanian option' in the tabloids and, at the elite level, in direct approaches to the king. Judging by past practice the Jordanian authorities could try to curb press freedom and contain political opposition.[6] There could be demonstrations and disturbances in the streets, triggering arrests. The net effect would be to oblige the Jordanian government to proceed with extreme caution. Probably, there could be no formal agreement between Jordan and Israel on *Functional* arrangements and power-sharing in the West Bank. Instead, there would be a *de facto* division of labour, which the Jordanian government could argue was temporary pending a better deal with the Israelis for West Bank Palestinians. Meanwhile, it could be possible for Jordan to extort some form of compensation and reward from Israel and from the United States for acquiescence. Certainly the situation would offer a source of leverage for increased economic support and there could be a security dimension.

It is conceivable that the United States would offer Jordan increased defence cooperation, involving transfers of equipment, joint exercises and training missions. On the economic front, Jordan might be offered more grant aid and official credits to help ameliorate the most painful consequences of economic restructuring in the name of liberalization. After all, in a situation of heightened political tension and uncertainty the chances of private and corporate investment would be diminished and Jordan would need more government assistance. In effect, the United States could develop a programme for economic and military support to Jordan to parallel its arrangements with Egypt, put in place following the signing of the Camp David accords, albeit on a lesser scale.

Economic factors and security constraints

The parlous state of the Palestinian economy could facilitate realization of the *Functional* scenario in the short run, but could well render

---

6 See Bassam Badareen, 'Confrontation seen looming between Jordanian government and opposition', in *al-Quds al-Arabi* (English translation in *Mideast Mirror*, 23 May 1997), where he argues 'the latest press curbs have raised fears about a general reversion to authoritarianism ahead of the [Jordanian] general elections [November 1997], and have unwittingly given a hitherto weak and divided opposition something to unite around.' See also Sama Kamal, 'Jordan: Election boycott', *Middle East International*, No. 555, 25 July 1997, p. 14.

it unsustainable in the longer term, given the security problems which would militate against closer integration between the Palestinians and either the Israeli or the Jordanian economy or both. Some deliberate measures would be required to overcome these problems.

Autonomy is an idea with a long pedigree. It was mooted as a solution for the Palestinian problem at the time of the Camp David Accords and Egypt–Israel peace treaty of the late 1970s. It was at the heart of the Shamir-Rabin initiative of May 1989.[7] According to the traditional logic of how it would work, it would take for granted the integration of the Palestinian economy with that of Israel. The alternative – the separation of the two economies – would require Israel to do without Palestinian labour and the Palestinians to attract inward investment to boost business activity and job creation within Palestinian areas. The Oslo formula was supposed to produce a measure of separation over time, but only in conjunction with the creation of industrial zones on the fringes of the Palestinian areas, where joint ventures between Israelis and Palestinians could be set up or Israeli contractors could continue to employ Palestinian labour, well away from Israeli population centres. *Autonomy-Plus* could involve a similar scheme. However, as of late 1997, the proposed industrial zones did not exist and security concerns made the atmosphere in Israel no longer conducive to the integration of the Palestinian workforce into the Israeli economy.

During the Palestinian Intifada, from the end of 1987 up to the signing of the Oslo accords, frequent strikes by Palestinian workers had eroded Israeli reliance on this source of cheap labour. Palestinian attacks on Israelis also raised fears about their presence inside Israel proper. However, it was not until 1993 that a major shift in attitudes occurred when a spate of knife attacks by Palestinians on their Israeli employers and others prompted the then Prime Minister Yitzhak Rabin to close off the West Bank and Gaza for an extended period, impeding traffic in goods and preventing Palestinian workers from

---

7 'A Peace Initiative by the Government of Israel', official text, published in *The Jerusalem Post*, 15 May 1989.

going to their jobs. In 1992 the number of workers regularly crossing 'the Green Line' was around 110,000.[8] With the advent of the 'closure' policy that number could be cut to nil for limited periods or be restricted to only a few thousand at others. In the meantime, the Israeli government allowed for the importation of guest labourers from Central Europe and the Far East to make up some of the shortfall. However, this recourse did not sit well with Israeli public opinion, especially when guest workers roamed around drunk in the streets or were found to be trying to stay permanently. The Likud leadership therefore promised in the 1996 election campaign to address the problem.

Because of his espousal of free market economics and liberalization, Netanyahu was expected to be more willing than his Labour predecessors to ease the constraints on Palestinian labourers. His rejection of a two-state solution to the Palestinian problem also implied that he could not reinforce the Israeli–Palestinian divide along the Green Line. Some commentators pointed out that this need not compromise his tough stance on security, since 'closures' did not prevent determined would-be bombers from sneaking in. However, the closure policy gave a sense of security to the Israeli public and it would have been politically risky for Netanyahu to abandon the practice in case more attacks ensued and he could be blamed for not doing as much as his predecessors to adopt all precautions. Consequently, Netanyahu continued the policy and in August 1997 implemented the toughest 'closure' ever, sealing off towns inside the West Bank from one another, closing border crossings to Egypt and Jordan, interrupting trade traffic with Israel and suspending payment of Palestinian tax dues to the PA.

This episode illustrates the potential of the Israeli government to exercise control over Palestinian economic fortunes. In that sense, Israel could impose *Autonomy-Plus* despite Palestinian objections. However, given the political impediments to using economic integration – and free movement of the labour force in particular – as an antidote

---

8 'UN Report Warns of Israeli Closure Policies on the Palestinian Economy', *ArabFile* (Newsletter of the Mission of the League of Arab States, London), Vol. 4, No. 2, July 1997, p. 7.

to Palestinian economic collapse, *Autonomy-Plus* could be very difficult to sustain. As mentioned previously, by 1997 the Palestinian economy was actually in worse shape than when the Oslo accords were signed. Inward investment expected as of 1993 was put at $2.49 billion over three years, but in fact amounted to only $1.35 billion.[9] A United Nations report estimated that the Palestinian economy had lost $6 billion between 1992 and 1996, mostly through loss of wages, trade revenues and uncollected taxes resulting from Israeli security closures. In summer 1997, unemployment had reached 40 per cent in Gaza and 31 per cent in the West Bank, according to Palestinian figures.[10] Per capita income also continued a downward slide in the West Bank between January 1996 and March 1997.[11]

Perhaps more important, at the strategic level the Palestinian economy has fundamental structural problems which would have to be addressed under *Autonomy-Plus* as under any other formula. A list compiled for a consultative document[12] for the European Union itemizes the economic obstacles facing Palestinian trade as follows:

(1) Small domestic market faced with competition from Israeli producers and exporters enjoying economy of scale, subsidies and financial incentives;
(2) Negligible infrastructure (energy, transport, telecommunications, water, financial);
(3) No direct access to third countries;
(4) All industrial and agricultural activity and all exports to Arab countries subject to licences by Israel;
(5) Unpredictable and restrictive practices as regards imports from outside Israel;
(6) Qualitative restrictions imposed by Jordan mainly on agricultural products;

---

9 *Ibid.*
10 David Harris, 'Builders ban all Palestinian labor', *The Jerusalem Post*, 1 August 1997.
11 *Ibid.*
12 Bernard Philippe, 'Triangle Palestine, Israel, Jordanie: Perspectives Offertes par le Libre-Echange avec L'Europe', D(97)PHILIBE\PUBLIC\PALESTIN\TRADPAP3, *Commission of the European Communities*, Brussels, 15 July 1997.

(7) No civilian judicial system, which makes it impossible to conduct/implement contractual agreements;
(8) Lack of statistical data;
(9) Disparities in the tax system;
(10) Major trade practices (pressure on EU importers not to import Israeli and Palestinian products at the same time);
(11) Poor transport conditions.

Given these factors, the Palestinian economy cannot survive without major changes. Dependence on Israel is a fact, which spells problems for Israel should it aim to implement *Autonomy-Plus* and still use the 'closure' tactic. Meanwhile, Jordan is also to some degree held hostage to Palestinian fortunes on the West Bank and cannot manage its econo-mic relations with the Palestinians in isolation from Israel, especially in the context of the *Functional* scenario, which, by definition, would involve no advancement on the Oslo process.

Oslo I, the subsequent Paris accords and the Israeli–Jordanian peace agreements ostensibly set the scene for multilateral economic cooperation between the Palestinians, Israel and Jordan. As it turned out, the results have fallen short of the original expectations. Leadership rhetoric has not been matched by action. A key problem lies with the terms of the agreements themselves. They are hidebound with stipulations and regulations affecting a whole list of categories of commodities which could be traded between Jordan, the Palestinians and Israel. The restrictions enable Israel to have a say in almost every aspect of bilateral commerce between Jordan and the Palestinian entity. This factor, together with the deleterious effect on business of Israeli security measures, has impeded free trade and undermined investor confidence in the near and long term. Overall, the PA has no real power to organize its external trade relations independently. On the Jordanian side, resistance to normalization with Israel translates into constraints on trading with the Palestinians.

Another concern is the lack of institutionalization in Jordanian–Palestinian business relations. There are no proper or permanent vehicles through which to handle coordination of detailed legislation implementing existing trade agreements. When it comes to defining the technical details of commercial relations, decisions are too often made in terms of political interests, not business needs. In many instances only those with experience in commerce and qualifications in economics are equipped to deal with the issues, but such expertise has been used only intermittently. At the level of dealings between the PA and the Jordanian government, almost every time the different parties have entered formal talks on trade relations, they have sent a different team of people, who have had to start from scratch.

The regional and international setting

Neither Egypt nor Syria would find anything to like in the *Functional* scenario. Egypt would be stuck with helping out the Palestinian leadership in Gaza, but would have difficulty making a case if Jordan facilitated the Israeli agenda for the West Bank. Syria would see an enhancement of Israeli power extending into Jordan. Fears that this arc of influence might one day extend to Iraq would be compounded. However, rather than face encirclement, Damascus could re-enter peace talks with Israel with renewed determination to get back the Golan and end the dangerous belligerence. Saudi Arabia's concerns about the future of Jerusalem would be heightened. However, the United States could give its blessing to the *Functional* scenario, if it looked like working, and the Europeans would be unable to redirect the dynamic.

Implications

As discussed in the preceding chapter, *Autonomy-Plus* could be all that the Palestinians get, by default rather than design. However, the *Functional* scenario necessarily implies an Israeli government that wants to make *Autonomy-Plus* work. On the face of it at least, there are certain security and ideological advantages to this as a policy which could make it saleable to sectors of the Israeli public. Given that there will be opponents to it within Israel, however, such a policy may have to be implemented by stealth. This implies the potential for an angry backlash inside Israel, especially if the policy founders.

Since Yasser Arafat and the PA cannot agree to *Autonomy-Plus* it will also fall to the Israeli government to ride out Palestinian objections. One way to do this would seem to be to undermine the authority of the Palestinian leadership. With the Oslo accords Israel opted for Arafat and the PLO as its principal partners in reaching an accommodation with the Palestinians. The PA was enabled to establish a police force to deliver on Israeli security needs and, as it turned out, at the expense of civil rights for the Palestinians themselves. Arafat's capacity to meet his side of the bargain has depended on Israel reciprocating, but *Autonomy-Plus* would fall too far short of Palestinian aspirations to meet the requirement. Consequently, the bargain would collapse and Israel would be in need of a new security partner. More than likely, it would look to Jordan to fill the gap.

It is possible to envisage, as attempted above, ways in which King Hussein could be drawn in, but only if he had Palestinian as well as Israeli and American backing. Even then, he would face considerable anger at home and from Palestinian nationalists and others. He would not have the backing of other Arab governments, quite the contrary. What is more, it is not clear how much Jordan could supplant Palestinian security cooperation with Israel inside the West Bank, let alone Gaza. It would take an enormous stretch of the imagination to envisage Jordanian security personnel taking up duties inside the West Bank. Once the cooperation of the PA was lost, it would therefore fall to Israel to make up the difference. Consequently, this scenario implies the possibility of Israeli forces having to re-enter areas under exclusive Palestinian control (Areas A under the Oslo formula), where they would be met with armed opposition.

The implications of the *Functional* scenario are therefore a weakening of Yasser Arafat, trouble for King Hussein inside Jordan and the possibility of armed confrontation between Israeli troops and Palestinians carrying guns. With the PA undermined, the way would be cleared for hardline factions, Islamist or secular, or both, to take greater prominence. This could amount to a self-fulfilling prophecy for those Israelis fearful of enabling the birth of a more warlike and dangerous Palestinian entity on their doorstep, if not actually in their midst. This would spell new dangers for Jordan too, which might persuade the Jordanian authorities to cooperate with the Israelis on containment of the Palestinian areas and border security. The big question then would be how to prevent the collapse of the Palestinian economy.

The only feasible way for the Palestinian economy to survive under the *Functional* scenario is for Israel and Jordan between them to provide an outlet. If, because of security concerns, Israel continues to resort to use of the closure policy, Palestinians will be cooped up in enclaves without enough business activity to generate full employment. International aid will not substitute for business confidence. Donor governments will baulk at handing over cash purely for immediate consumption and no lasting returns. Lack of a proper or enforceable regulatory framework will militate against private investment. Therefore, Israel would have to do something, such as the creation of industrial zones, to mitigate the situation. Jordan, meanwhile, would face a difficult choice: either opt for renewed confrontation with Israel, at least in political and economic terms, in the name of solidarity with the Palestinians, or find ways to help them with their immediate economic needs. The latter would involve encouraging businessmen on either side of the river to make the most of their opportunities for cooperation rather than isolation.

As will be seen in subsequent chapters, there is a business community in Jordan capable of linking up with its counterparts on the West Bank to develop better economic ties. Under the *Functional* scenario, Jordan would have to capitalize on the existence of this community as a lifeline to the Palestinians on the West Bank. Jordan would not be able to assist Gaza directly, so that task would fall to Egypt. But it could not help but play a role in the West Bank. The circulation of the Jordanian dinar there would be a key imperative. To protect the dinar Jordan would have to open its doors to more Palestinian products, to perpetuate such economic activity as exists in the Palestinian areas. Jordan would also be the conduit for more of the imports needed in the West Bank. The result would be a shake-up in the Jordanian economy, since some Palestinian products would undercut producers of the same goods in Jordan and although the

Jordanian government could perhaps redirect economic activity within its own borders it would not have the same direct powers in Palestine. There could be a reversion to some form of division of labour between producers on either side of the river Jordan, as there was between 1950 and 1967. The Palestinians could end up resentful at being the poor relations of Jordan, but on the East Bank there would be objections to having to accommodate West Bank needs.

In neither case could the government of Jordan afford to let market forces simply take their toll. Equally, it would not be in a position to mastermind infrastructure development to link in the West Bank and boost longer-term prospects there, because it would not have the political authority or the logistical access. In any case, the situation would require urgent measures just to prevent economic and financial collapse in the West Bank and there would be no time to wait for comprehensive infrastructure planning and development. The trend would nonetheless be towards a greater level of integration. Meanwhile, Palestinians in the West Bank would continue to look to Jordan to provide them with passports and an increasing number would be likely to seek relocation to Jordan.

Resistance to the *Functional* formula will come from Jordanian nationalists and from those sectors of the economy put at risk by West Bank competition. One of the implications of this scenario for Jordan, therefore, is heightened tension on the domestic front. This could well spell a security clampdown, putting at risk party politics, press freedom and further development of parliamentary democracy. The process of political party formation and maturation would be interrupted and redirected. Jordanian–Palestinian relations would take centre stage. Not all would be magnanimous in their treatment of this issue.

On the Palestinian side this scenario might have implications for national reconstruction efforts. On the one hand, Palestinians could rally around the flag and show support for the PLO leadership against Israeli and perceived Jordanian designs, and in pursuit of their national agenda and aspirations. In this case, Arafat might be able to maintain his popularity and power base without much resort to coercion. The development of political pluralism and party politics might not be derailed and press freedom could actually receive a boost. The political parties and factions would presumably focus on developing a response to Israeli and Jordanian policies first and foremost, and their relations with the PA would stem from this. On the other hand, some groups and individuals in the West Bank might seek to jump on the Jordanian bandwagon. The PA's response to this could take the form of coercion and the Palestinian political system might then take on a more authoritarian complexion. Broadly speaking, in the face of Israeli measures to undercut the process of state building, even if weakened, Arafat and the PA could count on Palestinian solidarity against Israel. The leadership might be more nervous, however, about the temptations for West Bankers to turn to Jordan.

In this highly complex setting, security issues would loom large for all the players. If there were a measure of peace, it would be peace by enforcement, not consent.

Outcomes

The *Functional* scenario could be the outcome of a deliberate Israeli strategy, with Jordan and Palestine swept along. This was how the scenario was envisaged above. However, it is also conceivable that it could come about by default, as the unintended consequence of failures to effect another outcome. Either way, it does not present an attractive proposition for all concerned.

The consequences of the *Functional* scenario could be a short-lived *de facto Autonomy-Plus* arrangement for the Palestinians in the West Bank and Gaza, which comes about in the late 1990s as a result of a fatal weakening of Arafat's position and the authority of the PA, together with Israeli determination to avoid conceding a Palestinian state. Jordan would have to be involved as a sort of life-line for West Bank Palestinians. In the absence of strategic moves by the Israelis and Jordan to address Palestinian citizenship rights and economic needs, the situation could disintegrate into *Breakdown* on the Israeli–Palestinian front and low-level warfare, with a potential for a new refugee crisis involving Jordan, and serious tensions if not strife within Jordan itself.

Alternatively, the *Functional* scenario might be made to endure somewhat longer, provided certain factors pertain.[13] Given the specifics of the disengagement process in 1988, King Hussein could conceivably reverse the disengagement and reinstate Jordanian citizenship for West Bank Palestinians. There is a certain Arab nationalist and Islamist constituency for doing so, and it is possible to imagine a situation in Palestine characterized by such despair (perhaps, as a result of Palestinian attacks, the Israeli army would reoccupy some of the evacuated areas and make clear that it planned no withdrawal in the near term) that increasing numbers of Palestinians might be convinced that this would be the best they could hope for.

The critical question then becomes not just whether West Bankers could be driven to accept such a plan, but whether the East Bank response would permit it. Among some Palestinian Jordanians the old suspicion of Hashemite intentions towards Palestine could be confirmed. Just as important, Jordanian nationalists could be expected vigorously to oppose such an outcome, for whatever the numbers of Palestinians versus Transjordanians currently resident on the East Bank, the effective incorporation of Palestinian population centres across the river would tip the balance overwhelmingly towards the Palestinians. To avoid a negative backlash, two sorts of Jordanian citizenship might be devised, one for East Bankers and one for West Bankers, or, perhaps, the maintenance of a kind of default or interim citizenship for Palestinians that would be administered by the Palestinian authorities in the West Bank in conjunction with the Jordanians. The first seems excessively artificial and in the long term an unworkable proposal. The second might be more easily accepted, but also seems unwieldy as a long-term arrangement.

In a *Functional* division of responsibilities, the formula with the greatest chance of enduring would be for Palestinians to retain positions of authority, albeit relying heavily on Jordan both for back-up and for weight in their dealings with the Israelis. It is well-nigh impossible to imagine a scenario in which Amman sends its own

---

13 The description offered here is drawn directly from a working paper prepared by Laurie Brand in consultation with Bassma Kodmani Darwish.

administrators into the Palestinian areas to govern them. The arrangement would be much less direct, but the dependence would be clear, in both political and economic terms.

In such a situation, whatever the form of citizenship, the future of Palestinian human and civil rights as well as the future of Palestinian civil society would depend upon their own administrators as well as the relationship with (and status of such rights in) Jordan, with the Israelis holding veto power in many instances. Political or civil rights could not be expected to develop any further in the West Bank than they would have in Jordan itself. Unless Palestinian nationalism is totally defeated and bankrupted by the process that leads to this outcome, it will, no doubt, require increasing levels of coercion to suppress.

It is most unlikely that the other principal actors in the region will remain quiescent in the face of this scenario. Such a Jordanian–Israeli condominium would pose a problem for the Syrians, one against which they could be expected to mobilize, probably causing problems for Jordan domestically. Egypt certainly has no interest in seeing Israel's regional strength bolstered by such an outcome. Finally, the Saudis could not be expected to chart an independent course from the Syrians and the Egyptians. This scenario does not, therefore, make for an ending of regional tensions.

A note on Jerusalem

On the Jerusalem issue, the *Functional* scenario would result in King Hussein retaining his role as custodian of the Muslim holy sites. International Christian bodies would retain their responsibilities at specific Christian sites, and the rights of Palestinians in respect of the holy sites would be subsumed under these and the Jordanian role. Israeli *de facto* sovereignty and political control would be undiluted in both East and West Jerusalem. Palestinians living within municipal Jerusalem and probably beyond, in 'Greater Jerusalem', would be obliged to become either Israeli citizens or Jordanian citizens with residence in Jerusalem. Jerusalem residency would be denied to any Palestinians without either form of citizenship.

4 THE *SEPARATION* SCENARIO

Separation is defined as the outcome of conscious decisions and deliberate steps to establish a Palestinian state (or entity) which, either by design or by default, is as separate and distinct from the Jordanian state as is possible. It could come about inadvertently, as a consequence of efforts by the Palestinians to do whatever is necessary to end the Israeli occupation, assert their independence and achieve sovereign status. Alternatively, it could be the result of a conscious choice to separate from Jordan, at the same time as achieve independence from Israel. It means that Palestine and Jordan would end up with separate and distinct legal, political, financial, educational and welfare systems. Infrastructure projects would be undertaken in isolation. Cooperation between the Palestinian and Jordanian leaderships would be minimal and both would generally deal separately with the Israelis. This scenario does not, however, preclude the two actors from forging closer links with third parties – for example, Palestine could grow closer to Egypt, and Jordan could grow closer to Israel, but the point is, their connections with each other would be limited.

The way *Separation* came about would affect the outcome. If, in the process of consolidating their independence from Israel, the Palestinians ended up also charting a course towards separation from Jordan, they might find themselves ultimately having to rely more on Israel, simply because they had disengaged from Jordan and could not easily look in that direction for cooperation. It is entirely feasible that *Separation* could come about in this way. Alternatively, however, separation from Jordan could be a central objective of the Palestinians, or perhaps more likely of their leadership, in the name of full independence. Palestinian distrust of the objectives of the Jordanian leadership, underscored by the events of the early 1970s, has never completely dissipated and could drive the Palestinian leadership to make separation from Jordan a deliberate and central goal. In that case the outcome would not come as a surprise, at least for the leadership.

What distinguishes the *Separation* scenario from the two other scenarios already considered is that elements on both the Palestinian and Jordanian side are assumed to take definite initiatives and act in accordance with a predetermined set of preferences which affect the future shape of their relationship. Under the *Drift* scenario, by contrast, neither Palestine nor Jordan proves capable of directing events in any systematic way. In fact, increased separation rather than cooperation could well be the result of *Drift*, but only by default. Under the *Functional* scenario, meanwhile, the Israelis are presumed to take the driving seat, while the Palestinians and Jordanians are swept along. The result of that, as was seen in Chapter 3, could be greater involvement of Jordan in the West Bank but again, not in accordance with a strategic plan chosen by the Arabs in advance.

The *Separation* scenario may be realized in stages. After all, Israeli acquiescence will be necessary for the Palestinians to achieve independent statehood in the West Bank and Gaza. But the scenario presupposes that the Palestinians, with Jordanian acquiescence, are set on a course which is leading towards a Palestinian state which is not only independent from Israel but also dissociated from Jordan, and which has a separate identity. Any thought of a confederation or some other form of political linkage with Jordan would presumably be set aside, either indefinitely or for good. Within the Jordan-Palestine-Israel triangle, eventually there would be three state actors of at least nominally equal status in terms of government-to-government transactions. The steps taken by the Palestinians and Jordanians on the way to that position will pull them apart rather than together and will put obstacles in the way of any third party, including Israel, which might prefer them to integrate.

Contributory and countervailing forces

While acknowledging that *Separation* could come about inadvertently, as one of the consequences of a Palestinian drive for sovereign independence from Israel, the discussion here will concentrate on how *Separation* could be realized by choice rather than default. It is possible to discern actors in Palestine and in Jordan for whom *Separation* would be the desired outcome. They will be the principal contributors to its realization by design; but they will be able to tap into the residual distrust of one another by Palestinians and Jordanians. The history of Jordan's role in the West Bank has led some Palestinians to suspect that Jordan could still aim to deprive them of total independence there. Equally, the legacy of events culminating in the PLO's showdown with the Jordanian authorities in September 1970, among other things, has left some Jordanians with the fear that the Palestinians might hope to make Jordan their own. Meanwhile, the ground has also been prepared for *Separation* as a result of Jordan's decision to disengage from the West Bank back in 1988 and the emergence of the Palestinian entity under the leadership of Yasser Arafat and the PA, spawned by the Oslo process.

Political leadership

Assuming *Separation* is a deliberate aim and not just an outcome of the Palestinian drive for independence from Israel, Yasser Arafat and the PLO are probably the political actors who will contribute most significantly to bringing it about. Given the experience of September 1970 and their expulsion from Jordan, the PLO leadership has obvious reason to harbour suspicions of the Jordanian leadership. Jordanian contacts with the Israelis over the years have fuelled PLO distrust. Meanwhile, as was mentioned in Chapter 3, the central objective of Arafat and the PLO is an independent Palestinian state in the West Bank and Gaza with a capital in Jerusalem. Their whole focus has been on dealing with the Israelis to this end. The PLO entered into the Oslo accords in secret, abandoning any pretence of 'Arab solidarity' with either the Jordanians or the Syrians. Arafat's own relations with Hafez al-Assad are so bitter that he can expect no real assistance from that quarter. His formal contacts with King Hussein, though more frequent than dialogue with the Syrian leadership, are still suffused with mutual suspicion. The only Arab leader to whom the PLO chairman is prepared to turn for support consistently and openly is President Mubarak, presumably because, from a PLO perspective, he can be counted on not to compete with its national agenda.

After the signing of the Israeli–Palestinian DOP in 1993, Jordan delayed another year before reaching its peace agreement with Israel, during which time the Israelis had to repair the damage done to their informal relations with King Hussein by their entry into the Oslo accords. After all, the Palestinian leadership was not the only one guilty of leaving the king in the dark and, through the DOP, Israel adopted the PLO leader as its chosen peace partner. The quid pro quo, of course, was that President Arafat and the PA deliver on Israeli security concerns and the Oslo formula gave them the tools to do this. Arafat's state-building exercise initially revolved around strengthening the Palestinian police force and bureaucracy, with minimum delegation of decision-making. In the process, a number of posts in the new administration were filled as much on the basis of loyalty to the president as talent or relevant experience. The overall effect, however, was to consolidate the position of the leadership.

Having 'chosen' the PLO leadership and its security apparatus, Israel would not find it easy to reverse that decision. As was seen in the last chapter, a hardline Israeli government could set about undermining President Arafat's position, but would be hard pressed to find a substitute for the Palestinian security forces to police the Palestinian community and thereby help to protect Israel. Meanwhile, in his leadership style, Arafat has shown no inclination to share his powers with rivals inside Palestine, let alone outside. Certainly, there have been instances when Arafat has benefited from a show of solidarity by the Jordanian leadership, as for example in autumn 1996 when King Hussein made a visit to Jericho as his guest. But the message sent by this episode was not only that the two were acting together, but also that the king had made a decision, for his own reasons, to give a boost to Arafat's position at that time.

Ever since Oslo, the Jordanian government has been almost studious in its avoidance of any direct involvement in dealings between the Israeli government and the Palestinian leadership. The Palestinians have not been consulted about Jordanian agreements with Israel, and their leadership was positively affronted by the provision in the Israeli–Jordanian peace treaty for King Hussein to retain a role of guardianship of the Muslim holy sites in Jerusalem. When the Palestinian president attempted in 1996 to replace the Jordanian Waqf employees at the Al Aqsa Mosque in Jerusalem with his own he was forced to back down in response to an angry reaction from the king. Since the Israelis recognize the king's role in Jerusalem, but have actually forbidden Arafat to visit the city and have allowed no formal PA presence there, the Palestinian president is not in a position to supplant King Hussein in this respect unless the Israelis change tack. The king's line, meanwhile, is that he will have a role in Jerusalem, as outlined in the Israel–Jordan Treaty, until such time as it can be transferred to the Palestinians. On the economic front, there has been minimal coordination between the Jordanians and the Palestinians over their separate arrangements with Israel. As was noted in Chapter 2, no provision was made for the Palestinians in the agreements on water reached between Jordan and Israel.

The factors which would influence King Hussein under the *Separation* scenario are closely related to those which were found to sway him under the *Functional* scenario. If Arafat becomes marginalized in the peace process and discredited with his people, it is likely it is that a vacuum will open up in the West Bank and that the king could be drawn in to fill it. The stronger President Arafat is, both in his dealings with the Israelis and in his standing within the Palestinian community, the less impetus there is for King Hussein to intervene. Consequently, realization of the *Separation* scenario depends to a considerable extent on Arafat and his leadership maintaining a commanding position.

Political systems

Oslo provided for the establishment of the PA and the election of the president and Palestinian Legislative Council. The process begun with Jordan's disengagement from the West Bank has thus been completed in terms of setting up a Palestinian political system which is separate from that of Jordan. The characters of the two systems are distinctive too. Through the PA and security apparatus, Arafat has created multiple and competing channels to the centre of power. In Jordan the monarchy keeps a balance between the different elements in the society.

In terms of their actual impact neither of the two legislatures wields much power, but for slightly different reasons. In the Palestinian case the parliament suffers from lack of attention while in Jordan the electoral system helps to control its composition. The elected Palestinian Legislative Council was not accorded the power to hold the executive fully to account. It has a mandate to legislate and thus it has an institutional interest in operating separately from Jordan and its Jordanian counterpart. The PLC therefore represents a force for *Separation*, but the process of dismantling the inherited legal infrastructure and constructing a new and distinctly Palestinian one has been slowed down by quarrels between the legislature and executive. Debate inside the Palestinian parliament has actually been very open, but so much so that the PA and Arafat in particular have sought to keep publicity for its proceedings to a minimum. The president is not obliged to act on PLC recommendations, including its call in August 1997 for the replacement of his entire cabinet. In so far as Arafat ignores what the PLC demands he fuels disillusionment with the political system.

In Jordan too there have been signs of disillusionment with the democratic system that the parliament represents. This is only partly to do with the powers of the legislature in relation to the executive. Of more concern in 1997 were the arrangements for the November elections. The Islamic Action Front (the largest political organization in the country) made a decision to boycott the elections and a few small opposition parties decided to follow suit, on the grounds that successive governments had resorted to heavy-handedness at the expense of democracy. The opposition voices pointed to two measures implemented constitutionally but undemocratically: first, the change in the electoral law in 1993, which reduced the number of Islamist deputies to almost half their strength in the 1989 election results; and, second, the change made to the press and publications law in 1997 which has forced some of Jordan's weekly newspapers out of business.

In Palestine, the third branch of government, the judiciary, is very much the vehicle of the president and has been used by him to reinforce separation. In Jordan the general impression is that the judiciary operates independently of the executive; due process is observed and the king cannot determine a court verdict, though he may pardon an offender after the courts have pronounced. In Palestine, however, summary justice has frequently been meted out by secret military tribunals which pass sentence within hours of arrests taking place. By weakening and marginalizing the formal judicial system and substituting other means of conflict resolution, traditional or otherwise, the PA leadership prevents the implementation of existing Jordanian laws in the West Bank, thus reinforcing separation. Meanwhile, it is the choice of the PA leadership that a whole new body of law be drawn up for Palestine which is separate from Israeli law, Jordanian law and any other law. Compatibility with the legal systems of either Israel or Jordan or even Egypt appears not to be a priority. The objective of the legislature in the PA, engaged in drawing up new regulations and legislation for the new Palestinian entity, is simply to embody the independence and separateness of that entity.

Three points are of relevance here for the *Separation* scenario. First, the links which bound West Bankers into the Jordanian political system have been formally ended with the abolition of seats for them in the legislature and the establishment of a separate Palestinian electoral process, for both a parliament and a president. Second, the way the two systems are structured and run gives the decisive power to the head of state, who, in the Palestinian case, is set on *Separation*. Third, residual links to Jordan through the legal infrastructure in the West Bank are being ignored or dismantled.

In the circumstances, Jordan becomes a passive bystander to what is happening to Palestinian laws. The legal system of Jordan, which used to pertain on the West Bank as well as the East before 1967, grew on top of the legacy of Ottoman law and then British Mandatory rule. After 1967, the West Bank came under Israeli military rule and regulations, but the Jordanian legacy was not eliminated. If the Palestinians proceed with a process of adopting a whole new set of laws, without regard to either the past or what exists in Jordan today, then a connection will be broken and an opportunity to forge compatibility deliberately forgone. This is *Separation* in the making.

Political parties

As was discussed in Chapter 2,[1] the political parties in Palestine have been in the process of adapting from their role during the struggle against occupation to their role within the Palestinian entity. Future relations with Jordan are not a pressing concern and the positions of the various parties and factions on this issue can only be extrapolated from their broad platforms. The PLO factions are committed to the slogan of confederation, in accordance with the official position of the Palestine National Council (PNC) articulated at Algiers in 1988. That said, there has been hardly any discussion of the issue since Oslo and it seems that Fateh generally assumes that it will be dealt with at the appropriate time by the appropriate authorities. The political culture of Fateh is to mobilize the Palestinians for the Palestinian national cause and because of its history, it is bound to be suspicious of Jordan. In any case, Fateh is the party of the regime. The leftist opposition parties, the DFLP and the PFLP, are if anything more favourably disposed towards *Separation* than Fateh.

Hamas, like the Muslim Brotherhood, has articulated no specific position on the subject, apart from coming out against King Hussein's 1988 disengagement from the West Bank. The general orientation of the Islamist trend is to favour unity in the name of unity of the *umma*

---

1 See Chapter 2 for a full appraisal of the different parties and trends.

(the community of all Muslims). However, this does not mean that these groups will definitely prevent a trend towards *Separation* provided they are not actually asked to endorse it as a goal, and it would be difficult for Hamas to condemn such a trend if it were camouflaged under the cause of Palestinian independence.

In Jordan, as has already been explored at some length, the question of Jordanian–Palestinian relations is of concern at two interrelated levels – as an issue of identity within Jordan and in terms of relations across the river. *Separation* would be very likely to suit the hardline Transjordanian nationalists, since it would enhance their prospects of asserting their identity in Jordan and provide a separate location to which Palestinian identity could be clearly relegated. Also, Jordanian political parties that are allies or offshoots of PLO factions would follow the PLO line on the quest for independence, which might embody separation in disguise. As of late 1997, this current is probably the dominant one in Jordan. Unlike in Palestine, however, those on the left of the political spectrum in Jordan are more ideologically inclined towards maintaining links with Palestine in the name of Arab unity. This puts them in the same camp as the Islamists, if only on the issue of future Jordanian–Palestinian relations.

President Arafat has been known to suspect King Hussein of using 'the Hamas card' or Islamist organizational links across the river to create difficulties in Arafat's path. This conspiracy theory has its proponents among Arafat's advisors, some of whom went so far as to claim that armed attacks on Israelis by Hamas, during the critical period in 1995-96, may not have been discouraged by the Jordanians, in an effort to undermine Arafat's role in the peace process to the benefit of both Jordan and Israel. The much less alarmist view is that King Hussein cannot dictate Hamas activities, but to the extent that the Palestinian leadership thinks he can, he has 'a Hamas card'. Meanwhile, Islamists and leftists could nurture their own links across the Jordan, which would cut across the *Separation* agenda and muddle the outcome. Alongside deliberately forged party political links, the informal family ties will be impossible to override completely.

Elites

The discussion on the role of political elites in the *Drift* scenario concentrated on those deriving their status directly from employment within the state apparatus, or 'state managers'. Obviously, this is not the only type of elite capable of influencing developments. In Palestine, three coalitions of social, economic and political elites are discernible. Traditionally the rich have been found in the commercial class which, on the West Bank, was historically pro-Jordanian and opposed to a separate Palestinian state. After Oslo the members of this class began reconciling themselves to the prospect and regrouping to take advantage of what the PA had to offer. Another coalition exists among the Palestinian bourgeoisie – the middle and upper-middle class which emerged during the 1960s and 1970s and controls the bureaucracy. The third grouping is the lower-middle-class, grassroots Fateh nationalists, who are in control of the security services. By 1997 alliances had begun to develop linking the rich commercial class and the members of the security apparatus to create economic ventures to mutual benefit. The national bourgeoisie is found doing business with Israel and (especially in Gaza) with Egypt.

On the Jordanian side, the elite within the state bureaucracy (which includes state enterprises and education) and the security services – where Transjordanians predominate – exists in parallel with a business elite, where there is a preponderance of Palestinians. Cutting across and connecting the two are alliances and coalitions between 'state managers' and private-sector entrepreneurs. This intermixing is evident in the composition of the boards of a number of public companies. Transactions in the West Bank are actively sought by contractors from Jordan, but often in order for the benefits to accrue on the Jordanian side of the river.

Attitudes towards *Separation* will obviously vary among elite members on either side of the Jordan. Family ties will override other considerations for some. Transjordanian nationalists may be guided first and foremost by ideology. However, almost by definition, 'state managers' may be expected to act in accordance with their interests in increasing the power and revenues of the state, and this will put the senior employees of the state in Jordan and Palestine in competition with one another, with little to gain and potentially something to lose from any process designed to amalgamate the two entities. Both will also probably see themselves in competition for the favours and financial support of outside powers, not least Israel, and the donor countries, principally the United States, Europe, Japan and the Arab Gulf states. On balance, therefore, state managers in Jordan and Palestine can be expected to go along with *Separation* and even help it on its way, whether consciously or unconsciously.

Civil society

Any mention of the term 'civil society' in the Arab context enters into a debate which has exercised many scholars because of differences of definition. For present purposes the term will be used in two ways.[2] Its more traditional use refers to professional associations and other NGOs aside from formal political groupings and state institutions which serve as a kind of buffer between the individual and the state. The other use of the term focuses on the rights of the individual as citizen rather than subject of the state. The mere existence of professional associations and other NGOs may not be sufficient to protect the rights of a citizen in the absence of an operative concept of citizenship. This concept implies that the citizen participates in the polity and has the ability to hold the state accountable. By contrast, if the individual is deemed a 'subject' of the state, this implies that his input is not significant and the notion of accountability need not pertain.

In Jordan the suspension or cancellation of martial laws and the reintroduction of parliamentary elections should have enhanced 'citizenship'. In fact, the state remains somewhat protected from direct accountability, since the upper house or senate is an appointed body and aspects of the budget have not been submitted for public discussion.

---

2 Developed by Laurie Brand in a working paper on 'Civil Society in Jordan and the Question of Jordanian–Palestinian Relations'.

More importantly, because of the communal divide in Jordan not every holder of a Jordanian passport is accorded the same citizenship status, at least in practice. Since the signing of the Oslo accords, it has been possible for some Transjordanians to envisage the emergence of a separate Palestinian entity where Jordanians of Palestinian origin could exercise their political rights in the future. This has enabled Jordanian nationalists to raise the concept of 'political return' and point openly to a segment of the population who should not have the same say as East Bankers in decisions about how they are governed in their place of residence. *Separation* would suit some East Bankers very well as a demarcation for 'political return'. The nationalists vary on which Palestinians might qualify for full citizenship of Jordan, but it is the idea of there being a choice which appeals.

With regard to the other facet of Jordanian civil society, among the professional associations a more inclusive definition of citizenship has surfaced in some cases. Since 1994 they have been in the forefront of resistance to 'normalization' with Israel, with the Writers' Association especially outspoken in its opposition. In fact, the quest to expand civil society in Jordan has become bound up with the campaign against normalization. Two groups, the doctors and the bar association, decided they wanted to allow West Bank members to vote in their elections, in the name of the campaign against normalization. The reaction of the government was to try to quash the results, though the issue was later dropped. Quite clearly, for whatever motives, the professional associations do harbour 'unionists' who would represent an obstacle to *Separation* at least so long as Israel also stood in the way.

In the case of charitable organizations engaged in development projects and improving the position of women in Jordan, these have made progress within their terms of reference, but more often than not they are bound in to the state in some way, through funding mechanisms and royal patronage, which increases their visibility and effectiveness in one sense while compromising their civil society function. In any case, they do not represent a decisive force for either *Separation* or *Cooperation*.

In Palestine the NGOs which operated under the occupation are divided on how to conduct themselves under the PA, and the situation has been complicated by the decision of some external donors to channel funds through the PA. Some Palestinian NGOs operate on the assumption that the Israeli occupation is over and have therefore switched their focus to relating to a Palestinian state in the making. Others are torn between working against the residual occupation and developing independence in relation to the PA. Broadly speaking, Palestinian NGOs are not conspicuous in their contribution to either *Separation* or *Cooperation*.

Refugees

Three-quarters of the Palestinian population of the Middle East live in the West Bank, Gaza and Jordan. Between them, Jordan, Palestine and Israel could solve the bulk of the problem of Palestinian citizenship status if they could agree, and their decisions would affect the prospects of refugees in Syria and Lebanon. Israel's stated position is clearly against implementation of the 'right of return' of Palestinian refugees to within the 1948 borders of Israel. Because the balance of forces on the ground favours Israel, the dominant view has been that the question of what to do with refugees and the so-called 'displaced persons' who fled to Jordan in 1967 revolves around the relative absorptive capacity of Jordan and the Palestinian entity or state and the views of Israel, as well as the question of compensation.

Pending resolution of all these questions, Jordan acts as a safety net for refugees there, for displaced persons and for West Bankers and even some Gazans in need of passports. However, West Bankers holding Jordanian passports do not have right of residence in Jordan. West Bankers with Palestinian passports can travel to Jordan on these, but Gazans in the same position must first obtain a visa. In 1989 Jordan switched from issuing five-year passports to West Bankers, to providing a document of only two years' duration, and then later to issuing five-year passports again. Meanwhile, laws applied by the Jordanian courts have not necessarily changed to reflect the 1988 disengagement. Consequently, in October 1997 the Supreme Court ruled that a West Bank Palestinian is in fact a Jordanian citizen who could not be denied a full five-year passport. In these complicated circumstances, it is no wonder that Palestinians and Transjordanians alike watch developments in this area with a measure of paranoia.

Separation as a goal would certainly not represent a panacea for all concerned. If formal *Separation* were in prospect, it would be necessary to work out who should negotiate with Israel over the fate of refugees – Jordan by itself, or the PLO, or both. The Jordanian leadership regards the issue of refugees as of strategic importance and the more real the possibility of *Separation*, the more likely the Jordanian leadership would be to demand involvement in decisions on the refugee question. Certainly, the fate of displaced persons would rest primarily with Jordan, and the possibility that Jordan could deprive them of their political rights and ask the Palestinian entity to accommodate them would affect Jordanian–Palestinian relations both inside Jordan and across the river. The question of the identity of all Palestinians in Jordan would be out on the table, giving rise to such uncertainty among Jordanians of Palestinian origin that a crisis could result with the potential to destabilize Jordan. Carried to its logical conclusion, *Separation* would cut off both refugees and displaced persons in Jordan if they could not relocate to the Palestinian entity.

In sum, Palestinian refugees and displaced persons in Jordan would be most likely to see *Separation* as contrary to their interests. Consequently, in trying to find a manageable way to resolve the refugee issue, the PA would run up against a serious obstacle to attaining *Separation*.

Public opinion and the media

Public opinion and the media will reflect the uncertainties and contentions surrounding the issues of identity and citizenship under the *Separation* scenario. The absence of an ideal solution helps to explain why indecision and thus *Drift* is a plausible scenario. However, assuming *Separation* is the goal of the Palestinian leadership at least, reactions among the public will depend on the prospects for a Palestinian state.

If there is little progress towards agreement between Israel and the

Palestinians on this, then the Palestinian populace will be forced to wonder what they stand to gain ultimately. As was seen in the previous chapter, if *Automony-Plus* appears to be all that the Israelis will concede for the present, then some West Bankers at least will look to Jordan to continue to provide a safety net. There would thus be a divide between aspirations and the dictates of practicality. The Palestinian media could be expected to put the case of the leadership for the goal of independent statehood, but individuals could not deliberately cut the ties with Jordan for the sake of realizing that goal, unless it approached reality. In Jordan *Separation* could get a favourable press precisely because it is embedded within the quest for Palestinian statehood, and it would have its supporters. However, public opinion would be divided on the benefits and penalties of *Separation* as and when its realization looked likely in the form of an actual Palestinian state accepted by the Israelis. Then all the difficulties of who should live where and with what passport would have to be addressed.

The Israel-Jordan-Palestine triangle

There is an Israeli constituency for a Palestinian state in the West Bank and Gaza, as was noted in the discussion about Israeli public opinion and political dynamics in Chapter 3. It consists of the very same elements who would stand in the way of realization of the *Functional* scenario. Of these, only some would have a clear position on whether the state should be as separate as possible from Jordan or linked to it. As was mentioned previously, Shimon Peres has harboured a preference for some form of 'Jordanian option' whereas Yitzhak Rabin seemed to be working on the assumption of separation, at least initially.

However, the outcome must depend on the kind and size of Palestinian state that Israel would agree to. If it were something along the lines of the *Fifty-Fifty* formula described in Chapter 1, there would be a *de facto* territorial split between Palestine and Jordan, reinforced by security arrangements. Without a contiguous border with Jordan, traffic between the East Bank and the West Bank could not move freely at the behest of only the Jordanians and Palestinians, since Israel would retain its presence in the Jordan Valley and at the various border crossings. Infrastructure projects could link Jordan and Palestine, but only with Israeli involvement. Goods passing from one to the other would cross Israeli territory or checkpoints and therefore Israel would want a say in customs arrangements.

Consequently, it would take a deliberate effort on the part of both Jordanians and Palestinians to forge links between them. Since, as was seen above, the Palestinian authority, and Arafat in particular, is inclined and moving in another direction, *Separation* is more likely than *Cooperation* to be the outcome, with a *Fifty-Fifty*-type solution on the West Bank. However, were the Israelis to concede something approaching the *Beilin-Abu Mazen* plan, Jordanian–Palestinian *Cooperation* would be that much simpler, as will be seen in Chapter 5. Of course, since *Beilin-Abu Mazen* would give the Palestinians considerably more than the *Fifty-Fifty* formula, Arafat and the Palestinians in general would be aiming for the former for its own sake. They could also aim for *Separation* under that deal and attain it, though with a contiguous border the informal links across the Jordan would survive more easily and render *Separation* less complete.

Economic factors

The economic factors in play will work both for and against *Separation*, whatever the deal the Palestinians may or may not achieve with Israel. An appraisal of the Jordanian and Palestinian economies reveals more similarities between them than contrasts. This could make them natural competitors.

The Jordanian economy is usually defined in terms of two main features: its relatively small size and the scarcity of natural resources. In the economic literature it is described as small and open in its regional context, with a price structure determined by the international milieu. It is structurally unbalanced in sectoral terms, with services accounting for two-thirds of GDP. The productive base in the industrial and agricultural sectors suffers from problems of both demand and supply. Among other factors, agriculture is affected by the limited amount of cultivable land, labour shortages in this sector, dependence on rainfall and a general shortage of water. Problems in the industrial sector include the relatively small size of industrial ventures, which limits their competitive capability. A combination of protectionism and the persistence of some monopolies and oligopolies further limits competitiveness, by reducing incentives to improve quality.

Jordan is at one and the same time open and protected. Because of its limited natural resources and small size, it cannot stand alone and is therefore exposed and vulnerable to external shocks. During the 1970s and 1980s it became largely dependent on regional export markets, initially in the Gulf and subsequently in Iraq. Economic pressures and changing political fortunes in these places have therefore rebounded on Jordan. In the meantime, especially during the 1970s, the government introduced a series of development plans to fuel growth, expanding the state sector to the point where public-sector corporations accounted for 17 per cent of GNP.

At the end of the 1980s, the Jordanian economy manifested a number of shortcomings at the macro level, including a state budget deficit, a trade deficit, a current account balance-of-payments deficit, a high level of external debt, a low level of savings, and a low ratio of savings to GDP. Jordan's foreign reserves were also at a low level. Since the devaluation crisis of 1988–89 obliged Jordan to submit to a structural adjustment programme in agreement with the World Bank and IMF, some improvements have been achieved as a result of considerable effort on the part of the state working in combination with the private sector. A reduction has been made in the state budget and current account deficits. Reforms enacted over the past several years to encourage investment have stimulated exports somewhat, opening up new markets, and some new industries have been established. The reform programme is set to run through to 1998 and the benefits of measures adopted thus far are only now becoming apparent. In the meantime, there is some impatience among the general populace to see tangible results.

In parallel with Jordan, the Palestinian economy is small and lacking in natural resources. True, its integration into the region is limited, but its dependence on Israel is pervasive. Since the establishment of the PA, there are signs of state intervention and protectionism emerging, even if, as yet, there is not the same level of interventionism as in Jordan. Public-sector cartels have gained charge of cement, fuel and cigarette sales, and have opted for stronger links with Israeli suppliers rather than Jordanian ones. In respect of oil derivatives, Palestine could clearly import more from the Jordanian refinery. Having initially insisted that any such imports should match Israeli standards, the Israelis have pronounced Jordanian products up to the mark. Yet the Palestinian orientation towards Israel persists, as much by default as by design. That said, Egyptian products have begun to show up in greater quantities in the Gaza Strip and, in some cases, such as chocolate, in the West Bank. This probably has more to do with traditional links between Gaza and Egypt, and the relative quality of Egyptian products, than with a deliberate decision to turn to Egypt rather than Jordan to substitute for Israeli suppliers. Even so, the close personal ties of Arafat and members of his immediate entourage to Egypt leave some room for speculation.

In practice there is a mark-up of over 100 per cent on goods from Jordan as a result of the logistical problems of transporting them. The bridge across the Jordan is built to bear a maximum load of only 20–25 tons and the average cement truck weighs 35 tons when full, which means that passage can only be made by unloading and reloading the cargo on either side. In addition, the Israelis still insist on physically inspecting everything, rather than relying on electronic searches. Potentially, the new surveillance equipment pledged by the United States in 1996 can reduce this problem, but even so, the paperwork required, numerous fees to be paid and added labour and time considerations represent a deterrent to increased trade across the river.

Another phenomenon has emerged since the opening up of the crossing between Jordan and Israel in the north. Some goods are apparently being imported by Israelis from Jordan and then sold on in the West Bank at a profit. Since the market for such goods is limited in Israel itself, typically as soon as they arrive they are routed straight to Jenin in the north of the West Bank. Also, the peace agreements have failed to produce the independence from Israeli agencies that Palestinian sub-agents of foreign suppliers were hoping for. Foreign companies, such as Mitsubishi, have persisted in using their Israeli agents as intermediaries and, recently, even Jordanians, rather than deal direct with agents in the West Bank. It is quite feasible for Jordanians of Palestinian origin to open outlets in the West Bank as an extension of their Jordanian operations, and their West Bank customers are often unaware that this is the arrangement.

In the financial sector Palestinians are unhappy about the operations of the banking system since the peace agreements. Banks newly opened in Palestine are quite likely to transfer deposits across the river to Jordan, apparently denying the Palestinian economy the benefits of increased investment facilities there. According to some sources, as little as 20 per cent of bank deposits in Palestine is invested locally, but others would dispute this figure. Perhaps the issue here is a psychological one, in that the opening of branches of Jordanian banks has been one of the few visible signs of interest in the Palestinian economy, which does not represent the same sort of vote of confidence that opening a factory would, especially if some proportion of the funds is transferred out. From a Jordanian perspective, the biggest concern is the vulnerability of the dinar to the vicissitudes of the Palestinian economy. True, the Palestinian Monetary Authority is monitored by the World Bank and IMF, but since perhaps 25–30 per cent of the total value of the Jordanian dinar in circulation resides in the West Bank – the total value being about 1–1.2bn dinars in 1996 – the Jordanian Central Bank is bound to be wary. The spectre of the run on the dinar of 1988–9 is still fresh in popular memory.

There has been almost no transnational coordination on infrastructural arrangements in the Middle East as a whole, and Jordan and Palestine are no exception. Each country has concentrated on developing its own systems, leading to fragmentation, duplication and unnecessary expense, all to the detriment of regionwide economic development. In the absence of a comprehensive railway system and other forms of mass transport, there is heavy dependence on individual forms of transportation.

Plans for infrastructure development in Palestine look set to bolster *Separation* rather than encourage cooperation with Jordan. It seems the decision has already been taken to build a new airport in the West Bank as well as the Gaza Strip, pending Israeli acquiescence. Even if one can be justified in the Gaza Strip, for the West Bank arrangements could be made to use Jordan's facilities, at least for the immediate term. It is politics which interferes with logic here. In part, Israel is to blame, but the PA has been making the running on such issues. With respect to electrical power the Palestinians have been intent on building their own power station as soon as possible rather than making any use of what Jordan could supply. Estimating the price of providing one kilowatt at $1,000, it is fair to assume an investment of $150m over four years for the prospective Gaza plant.

Along with cement, oil products were included in Category A of the list of commodities drawn up in the trade agreements between Israel, Jordan and Palestine. With Israel's pronouncement that Jordanian derivatives were meeting its standards, this should have opened the way for the Palestinians to turn to Jordan for fuel and other oil products. However, this has not happened. Pipeline links across the river would be relatively easy and cheap to build, and the possibilities have been discussed between Jordan and Palestine. What is needed is a deliberate move by the Palestinians to shift a proportion of their import requirements from Israeli to Jordanian suppliers; without this, *Separation* from Jordan, at the expense of greater reliance on Israel, will prevail.

The regional and international setting

International donors have made known their preferences for intra-regional development schemes, but in the absence of formal proposals they cannot insist. Instead, the international community is awaiting more progress on the political front, in particular between Israel and the Palestinians and between Israel and Syria. Neither the United States nor Europe has made any specific pronouncements on how it would like to see Jordanian–Palestinian relations progressing. The United States has focused on keeping the Israeli–Palestinian track of the peace process alive, leaving other questions for resolution later.

When US Secretary of State Madeleine Albright made her first visit to the region in September 1997 it was in an atmosphere of crisis, following the two sets of attacks by Palestinian suicide bombers in Jerusalem and the stringent Israeli security clampdowns. Albright did call for a 'time out' in Israeli settlement-building to improve the atmosphere for peace talks to resume, but the Israeli premier ignored this when calling for an expansion of the Efrat settlement following her visit.[3] US objections to this notwithstanding, the impression has prevailed among both Palestinians and Jordanians that the United States is too partial to Israeli interests to act as a neutral mediator in the peace process. In fact, by mid-1997, distrust of the US role had gone beyond concern about its bias towards Israel, and the United States was actually seen as a complicating factor in the quest for peace.

This perception was apparent across the Arab world. Meanwhile, the Arab players in the region have no interest in promoting Jordanian–Palestinian cooperation; quite the contrary, as was seen in the *Functional* scenario. Consequently, Syria would pose no obstacle to *Separation* and Egypt could be positively supportive, though both have been more preoccupied with the dangers of a total collapse in the peace process as a whole.

Implications

From the perspective of President Arafat and the PA, *Separation* is already on the agenda. There is no power-sharing between the Palestinian and Jordanian executives, legislatures and judiciaries. A separate body of Palestinian law is in the making. Decisions have been made to develop the Palestinian infrastructure without regard to Jordan.

One of the principal implications of this trend towards *Separation* is an inbuilt necessity for Palestine to retain, if not extend, its dependence on Israel. Realization of the ultimate goal of independent Palestinian statehood depends entirely on Israel agreeing. If negotiations with

---

3 Margot Dudkevitch and Marilyn Henry, 'US slams Netanyahu over Efrat expansion', *Jerusalem Post*, 26 September 1997.

Israel fail to produce anything more than a *de facto Autonomy-Plus* for the Palestinians, then *Separation* could prove a hollow victory. The PA simply could not provide all the attributes of statehood, such as a currency and passports, so a role for Jordan would still exist. If negotiations produced a *Fifty-Fifty* solution, the separation of Palestine from Jordan would be geographically reinforced. However, since the Palestinian economy cannot function in isolation, reliance on Israel would be that much greater if ties to Jordan were rejected on political grounds. Egypt would no doubt play an important role as a supplier and outlet for Gaza, but only courtesy of Israel for the West Bank. Israelis could extend the practice of buying Jordanian goods to sell on to Palestine at a mark-up. If, however, the Palestinians succeeded in getting a deal out of Israel which resembles the *Beilin-Abu Mazen* plan, replete with a contiguous border with Jordan, then *Separation* could also pertain, but would require deliberate reinforcement at the political level, to minimize the amount of traffic of all descriptions between Jordan and Palestine. Again, the Palestinians would have to look to Israel and Egypt for their economic lifeline if Jordan were deliberately ruled out.

On the security front, the Palestinian Authority would have to deliver on Israeli requirements in order to retain the role of sole partner to the Israeli government in peace negotiations. Hitherto, this has meant undercutting civil rights in the interests of bolstering police powers. The Palestinian leadership would therefore face the problem of Palestinians comparing their political system with those of their neighbours, including Jordan, and possibly drawing unfavourable conclusions. The onus would be on the PA to show that *Separation* could not only fulfil aspirations for independence but also produce material benefits in the longer term. It is to be expected that Palestinian families linked across the Jordan will not sever their connections and will render *Separation* somewhat incomplete.

Perhaps most importantly, it is not clear how *Separation* could address the problems of refugees and citizenship for Palestinians in Jordan to the satisfaction of all sectors of the two communities. Assuming the Palestinians attained some sort of a state and could issue formal citizenship, nonetheless it would find it extremely difficult to accommodate all the Palestinians living in Jordan, assuming they wanted to return or Jordan wanted them out. Jordan would either have to devise a residency status for Palestinian citizens there, which might leave a whole sector of that population only half enfranchised, or make them full citizens, which would be contrary to the ideological preferences of Transjordanian nationalists. In either case, Jordan would still have an identity problem and would still have to take Palestine into account in its internal as well as regional affairs.

Outcomes

On the assumption that the peace process does remain in play, some prognoses are possible. Given all the obstacles, after two or three years of Palestine and Jordan pursuing *Separation* and the Israeli government pursuing its own agendas, the outcome will probably be contrary to intentions. The moment *Separation* became explicit, Jordan could turn round to the Palestinians and inform them that if this was their choice, Jordan need no longer shoulder any responsibilities for the Palestinian cause. Indeed, it could serve notice on the Palestinian leadership that henceforth Jordan would treat Palestine as 'just another Arab country'. In effect, the Jordanian message to the Palestinians would be that they could not have their cake and eat it too! If they insist on being on their own, they must bear the consequences.

For some Transjordanian hardliners and for Palestinian advocates of *Separation,* realization of this scenario would spell political victory. However, *Separation* does not offer any easy solutions to the questions of refugees, citizenship and passports. When they came to tackle these, the Jordanian and Palestinian leaderships would have a hard time satisfying the conflicting demands. Israel would obviously have to be involved in such negotiations, if the issue of 'right of return' was to be settled.

During the transition, the Palestinian economy would continue to flounder and separation from Jordan would produce no benefits on this score. The Palestinians would have to hope for increased access to jobs in Israel and the implementation of schemes for industrial zones.

If they got these, it would mean greater reliance on Israel and heightened economic competition with Jordan, which would undermine mutual trust and goodwill. Alternatively, if the Palestinians did not achieve better economic cooperation with the Israelis, their situation would deteriorate and in the name of solidarity, some Jordanian businessmen and professional organizations could still hold out on normalization with Israel. As a result Jordan and Palestine would both suffer. In the near term as well, Jordan would still be hostage to the fate of Palestine because of a shared currency.

The conclusion on *Separation* is thus that it offers clear political advantages to elements on both sides, but spells economic drawbacks. Even so, many of the economic problems will exist whatever the scenario, and to overcome these will require deliberate decisions to minimize Jordanian–Palestinian competition. A commitment to political *Separation* could, ultimately, smooth the path to economic coordination. So, in the end, after two or three years in pursuit of *Separation*, Jordanian–Palestinian relations could either dissolve into acrimony and shared economic gloom or they could flourish on the basis of political separation and economic coordination. In either case, so long as Israel and the Palestinians achieve some agreement on final status issues, Jordan and Palestine will end up with separate executive, legislative and judicial systems, separate legal and security arrangements and, in the Palestinian case at least, the results could deal a serious blow to aspirations for democracy.

A note on Jerusalem

Under the *Separation* scenario, if Israel agrees, the Palestinian Waqf would take over control of the Muslim holy sites in Jerusalem. If Israel insists that this can only happen if the Palestinian Waqf is subordinated to the Jaffa Islamic Court, then the Palestinian leadership will presumably prefer that King Hussein retain his role of custodian. A larger role for the Palestinians in the handling of Christian issues will also depend on Israeli acquiescence. Whatever sovereign or political rights, if any, are ceded in Jerusalem by the Israelis will pass to the

Palestinians.[4] Again assuming Israeli agreement, Palestinian Jerusalemites will hold Palestinian passports, and if denied this they would take it upon themselves to seek special status as citizens of an international city. The Israelis can be expected to continue trying to curtail or reduce the number of Palestinians with residency in Jerusalem. The extent of Palestinian municipal rights, control of building permits and so on would depend on the Israeli position. The main point here, however, is to demonstrate that under *Separation* King Hussein would be expected to defer to the Palestinians on how much, if any, involvement he should retain in the affairs of the city.

---

4 Under the blueprint drawn up by Yossi Beilin and Abu Mazen, Yerusaleim (i.e. West Jerusalem) would be the Israeli capital; Al Quds (i.e. Abu Dis) would be the Palestinian capital; Jerusalem (i.e. Palestinian neighbourhoods around the walls of the Old City) would be under Palestinian autonomy; and the status of the Old City would remain a frozen issue for ten years, with the exception of the Al Aqsa compound, which would be under Palestinian sovereignty. For further elaboration, see Chapter 1.

5 THE *COOPERATION* SCENARIO

The *Cooperation* scenario is about precisely what it implies. It examines the prospects for and implications of cooperation between Jordan and Palestine. In parallel with the *Separation* scenario, it looks at *Cooperation* as both a process and an objective. It assumes that cooperation is possible, under certain conditions, as a *modus vivendi* pending the outcome of negotiations with the Israelis about the final status issues pertaining to the Palestinians. It also looks at how *Cooperation* could work as an objective *after* final status issues have been settled. However, there are problems in reconciling these two permutations of the scenario. Any decision to cooperate before final status arrangements are in place will influence the way final status issues are tackled. It could impede progress or facilitate it, but will certainly raise fears in the two communities that they are victims of a plot for unification. Consequently, it may require a crisis to persuade Palestinians and Jordanians to cooperate in the near term, as will be discussed.

In total, this scenario posits five forms or levels of cooperation between Jordan and Palestine as a result of deliberate choice by the leaderships. Under the circumstances pertaining in the autumn of 1997, it is possible to envisage a level of cooperation that does not approach merger, which will be called *cooperation under present circumstances*. Given the establishment of a Palestinian state, however, cooperation could take the form of *coordination between two states*. The other versions of the scenario which do envisage something approaching merger assume that the prior establishment of an independent Palestinian state is an essential precondition. These forms of the cooperation scenario are *confederation*, *federation* and *unity*.

The very mention of the word 'unity' creates difficulties for dispassionate discussion of the *Cooperation* scenario and its various permutations. However, what is suggested here is a set of frameworks for exploring the implications of different levels and types of cooperation between Jordan and Palestine, in the interests of clarity and constructive thinking. The distinctions may be useful for deciding how much is enough in the way of cooperation! The intention is not to advocate any one of the outcomes discussed, though a case is made for the benefits as well as the pitfalls for more cooperation than has been attained hitherto.

Contributory and countervailing forces

As will be obvious from the discussion in previous chapters, *Cooperation* has been conspicuous by its absence from Jordanian–Palestinian interactions. This scenario therefore requires a more deliberate effort of will, in place of the inertia on all sides which characterizes the *Drift* scenario, the submission to an Israeli agenda which underlies the *Functional* scenario, and an inclination or tendency to go separate ways manifest in the *Separation* scenario.

Political leadership

As was discussed at length in Chapter 4, the Palestinian leadership is principally a force for *Separation,* not *Cooperation.* It may well be the case that it sees cooperation as a danger to the potential gains to be derived from separation. President Arafat certainly appears to want to consolidate an independent power base before discussing relations with Jordan in any detail. However, if he sensed his situation weakening, it would not be beyond him to seek some assistance from Jordan. By way of illustration, Arafat has welcomed consultations with King Hussein when the Israeli government has done something which undercuts his objectives. For example, he went to see the king in the midst of the crisis in Israeli–Palestinian relations following the Mahane Yehuda bombing.

Since the Palestinian leadership clearly does not want to find itself subordinate to the Jordanian leadership, or Palestine to end up an appendage of Jordan, the only benefit it would be likely to consider worth having from the Jordanian side would be support for its objectives for Palestinian statehood, irrespective of the eventual relationship to be worked out between Jordan and Palestine.

For the Jordanian leadership, meanwhile, there has been little incentive to work closely with the Palestinian leadership so long as it has been pursuing its own independent agenda with the Israelis with some success. As was seen in Chapter 2, King Hussein has good reason to remain somewhat aloof and await developments. If Arafat and the PLO make headway, then there is likely to be little Palestinian support for his intervention. If Arafat and the PLO founder, however, the king could actually be asked to help and would therefore enter the arena with more room for manoeuvre. In the meantime, the mutual suspicion between King Hussein and President Arafat is such that they will not make natural partners.

The kind of crisis in developments which could change the calculations of both these leaders was posited in the *Functional* scenario. As was suggested there, if the Israelis were to be set upon forcing a *Functional* division of labour on the West Bank and denying the Palestinians anything more than *Autonomy-Plus*, they would have to weaken the position of Arafat and the PLO and draw King Hussein into the political vacuum which would result on the West Bank. If the crisis went deep enough, and Israeli forces re-entered some Palestinian cities, there could be a new refugee crisis, which would put Jordan in the difficult position of having to either accept more Palestinians within its borders or forcibly exclude them.

Under these circumstances, the Palestinian leadership would have little to lose and much to gain from Jordanian support, provided that support was about strengthening the Palestinian hand, not taking advantage of the situation. For its part, the Jordanian leadership could argue that support for Palestinian statehood, albeit with a measure of *Cooperation* at a number of levels, would be preferable to the political chaos which could ensue from a collapse of the Palestinian cause, leaving Jordan as the only outlet for the West Bank.

It does not seem possible that King Hussein could contemplate a return to the pre-1967 situation with the West Bank merged into Jordan. That would dash Palestinian aspirations and meet with fierce opposition from Transjordanians afraid that Jordan would eventually be turned into Palestine. Consequently, *cooperation* with the Palestinian leadership could represent a preferred course of action *under present circumstances*. In other words the Palestinian and Jordanian leaders could choose cooperation with each other as a mechanism for avoiding something more dangerous to them both. *Cooperation under present circumstances* could thus mean developing a common vision on final status issues, in part as a way to strengthen the bargaining position of the Palestinians with the Israelis and other third parties.

An explicit Jordanian endorsement of the Palestinian objective of independent statehood would help assuage fears on both sides. It could also be stipulated that this would be the prerequisite for any subsequent form of cooperation, whether *cooperation between two states*, *confederation*, *federation* or *unity*.

Such ultimate objectives need not be discussed in detail, however, pending settlement of the final status issues. Yet it would be logical for the two leaderships to proceed in a manner designed to keep all options open for the future, and this implies a departure from the dynamic underlying the *Separation* scenario. It suggests the value of making sure that the Palestinian system-in-the-making is compatible with that of Jordan. If nothing else, compatibility between the two legal systems and regulatory frameworks would facilitate economic cooperation. As was seen in the previous chapter, incompatibility and competition between the two economies are more in evidence than harmony and cooperation under present circumstances. To overcome this would require not only leadership initiatives but coordination at other levels between the two societies.

Elites

If a crisis is what is needed to change leadership thinking, the impact will obviously go beyond just the leadership. Supposing the circumstances of Palestinians inside Gaza and the West Bank progressively deteriorate in political, economic and security terms, a constituency for merger with Jordan could take shape. Union with Jordan might have more appeal than *Autonomy-Plus*, with Palestinian internal affairs run by an emasculated but assertive Palestinian Authority and security apparatus. Depending on the level of economic cooperation on offer with the Israelis under *Autonomy-Plus*, the Palestinian business elite might see more to be gained from attachment to Jordan. Some of the old West Bank socio-economic elite who used to thrive under Jordanian rule could hope for a revival of status. However, these elements would probably be outnumbered or overshadowed by those who would not consider anything approaching merger without the prior creation of an independent Palestinian state.

Those who would stand to lose from merger with Jordan, even as a last-ditch option, would be the senior 'state managers' of the Palestinian Authority and the security chiefs. Any of those who had established beneficial arrangements with Israeli contractors and suppliers would clearly be against a change of circumstances, even if they had to put up with only *Autonomy-Plus* as the alternative for the foreseeable future. On the Jordanian side it is likely there would be many more opponents of any kind of merger among the various elites. Ever since the Oslo process got under way, the members of the Jordanian elite have been free to plan their futures in Jordan without fear of having to share power with West Bankers, on the assumption that they would be provided for in the Palestinian entity. The most virulent opponents of any link-up with the West Bank would be Transjordanian nationalists, of course, both in the elite and at the popular level. For them the mere notion would be nightmarish.

On the Jordanian side at least, therefore, any moves towards Jordanian–Palestinian cooperation would have to be presented as a mechanism for enhancement of Palestinian chances of achieving independence rather than a prelude to closer association in political terms. That is why the *Cooperation* scenario cannot envisage cooperation along the lines of confederation, federation or unity without the prior establishment of an independent Palestinian state. It is also why it is possible to envisage a form of *Cooperation* between the Jordanians and Palestinians, in the immediate term, if it enhances the chances of the Palestinians standing up to the Israelis.

Turning to what might happen after attainment of Palestinian statehood, there would certainly be an intellectual constituency for closer links between Jordan and Palestine. There are very real concerns that the Palestinian entity is evolving into an authoritarian system. A link-up with Jordan could be seen as a way of countering or ameliorating that prospect, if it reinforces the institutionalization of decision-making powers and promotes efficiency and accountability. On the Jordanian side, within an important sector of the elite, there is a general sense that there has been a regression in the democratic process since 1993. There is also the issue of discrimination felt by Palestinians in Jordan. Thus, campaigners for pluralism and accountability in public life could join forces across the Jordan and capitalize on one another's strengths and experience to promote reforms in both systems. However, vested interests in the two systems, especially those of 'state managers' and sectors of the commercial elite, would be threatened. These elements would stand in the way of any form of merger.

Political parties and public opinion

Similarly, at the popular level, the two biggest obstacles to Jordanian–Palestinian *Cooperation* are the fears of both Palestinians and Jordanians, for opposite and contradictory reasons, regarding unification. On the Palestinian side, anything which smacks of a return to pre-1967 arrangements between the West Bank and Jordan spells a denial of Palestinians' self-determination, a negation of their distinctive nationalism. On the Jordanian side, the fear is that Jordan might thereby be turned into Palestine, by sheer weight of numbers. On both sides the perception exists that the more Jordan and Palestine cooperate voluntarily, the more the Israelis might be encouraged to think that Jordan can provide the solution to the Palestine problem.

It is to be expected, therefore, that Fateh and other factions of the PLO, notably the PFLP and DFLP, will resist *Cooperation*. Their opposition will be matched, if not outdone, by the nationalists in Jordan. However, as was seen in Chapter 4, the left-wing Arab nationalist trend in Jordan will be more likely to see the advantages of *Cooperation* in the long term. The Islamists on both sides of the river will meanwhile go along with *Cooperation* as an expression of the proper conduct of Arab Muslims working towards the greater good of all Muslims in the region. Since the Islamists place the greatest emphasis on opposition to the Israelis, they will rally to a cause designed to confront enduring Israeli control over the West Bank and Gaza.

In mid-1997 the Jordanian political scene was dominated by a confrontation between some opposition groupings — including Islamists, leftists, some centrists and professional associations — and the government of Prime Minister Abdul Salam Majali over the nature of the electoral law, the press and publications law and a general sense of political regression. Although it would not be possible for these groupings to oppose *Separation* if this were camouflaged under the banner of Palestinian independence, they could support *Cooperation* given the necessary conditions.

The attitudes of the public in general are complex combinations of sometimes seemingly contradictory aspirations laced with residual fears. The findings of a joint poll[1] conducted by the Center for Strategic Studies in Amman and the Center for Palestine Research and Studies in Nablus in October 1995 offer some pointers. The pollsters specifically asked whether respondents would agree that the relationship between Jordanians and Palestinians was unique and special, and differed from the relationship between those peoples and any other Arab people. In Jordan 92 per cent agreed to the proposition and among Palestinian refugee-camp dwellers in Jordan the proportion agreeing was 95.5 per cent. In the West Bank 84 per cent of respondents agreed and in the Gaza Strip those agreeing totalled 77.5 per cent.

---

1 *Jordanian–Palestinian Relations: The External Dimension*, CPRS and CSS, October 1995, pp. 3–4.

Table 1: Preferred form of unity (%) as expressed in opinion poll, 1995

	Confederation	Federation	Unity	None of these
Jordan	18.9	9.5	51.8	13.6
Camps in Jordan	16.1	8.2	68.6	5.5
West Bank	44.7	6.4	22.8	23.7
Gaza Strip	53.7	4.8	15.1	23.5

In response to a question about whether they would support any form of unity between Palestine and Jordan in the context of their future relationship, 86 per cent of the national sample in Jordan said yes and among camp dwellers 94.7 per cent agreed. In the West Bank 77 per cent said yes, and in Gaza 77.5 per cent. However, when queried about specific forms of unity, namely confederation, federation or unity similar to the pre-1967 order,[2] the breakdown of responses was as shown in Table 1 above.

Until further polls are taken asking the same questions in the contemporary setting,[3] it is not possible to know how much public opinion may have changed since October 1995 and it may be assumed that responses at any time will reflect levels of optimism and pessimism about the peace process. In any case, the findings in 1995 would seem to substantiate the view that West Bankers and Gazans want independence first and foremost, and a constituency for cooperation with Jordan to the extent of a confederation exists on this premise.

Surveys undertaken specifically among students in the West Bank and Gaza have revealed a majority in favour of separation from Jordan. However, the size of the majority was found to fall[4] in the aftermath

---

2 The terms were not defined in detail for the purposes of the survey and are not to be confused with the definitions spelled out for these terms at the end of this chapter.
3 CPRS and CSS are expected to conduct a joint poll at the end of 1997, which will provide data to compare with the 1995 findings. The new poll will also survey public opinion on each of the scenarios explored in this book.
4 Research conducted by CPRS.

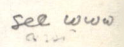

of an incident on the West Bank in March 1996 when Palestinian police entered universities and harassed and arrested students apparently for opposition to PA policies, especially on the peace process. This finding serves to illustrate the point made previously that when esteem for the PA falls for some reason, the idea of closer links to Jordan gains some appeal. However, Palestinian public opinion would react negatively to any suggestion that Palestinian nationalism be sacrificed in the process.

In February 1995 the Center for Strategic Studies conducted a survey designed to identify the type of relationship existing between Jordanians and Palestinians inside Jordan, how they saw each other and their mutual fears.[5] It also aimed to identify factors which impeded integration and determined the level of polarization in society. The survey further attempted to see what type of future relationship Jordanians and Palestinians in Jordan envisaged for Jordan and Palestine. When asked what kind of links they would prefer to see in the future, a majority wanted some form of unity with the West Bank; however, the proportion was higher among Jordanians of Palestinian origin.[6] The findings also revealed both a level of polarization and a high level of integration between Jordanians and Palestinians in Jordan. Two key fears of Transjordanians came out clearly – namely, fear of becoming a minority in their own country, and fear of the consequences of what many perceived as the dominance of Palestinians in the private sector. They apparently felt that Palestinians held dual loyalties and generally failed to appreciate what they had been able to achieve in Jordan. For their part, Palestinians in Jordan saw obstacles to integration in the predominance of Transjordanians in the public sector, their presence in sensitive senior positions in the state and the fact that Palestinian representation in both the government and the parliament fell short of reflecting their numbers in society.

Against this background, it is possible to conclude that any form of *Cooperation* which goes beyond either *cooperation under present circumstances* or *coordination between two states* must attempt to resolve Transjordanian

---

5 CSS Survey, *Jordanian–Palestinian Relations: The Domestic Dimension*, February 1995.
6 *Ibid.* p. 22.

fears in some way[7] at the same time as recognizing Palestinian national aspirations by making independent statehood a prerequisite.

Economic factors

In Palestine, popular antipathy to any new ventures with or increased dependence on the Israelis does set the scene for expanding Palestinian–Jordanian trade and cooperation. Certainly there is a manifest desire in the West Bank to turn to Jordan to supply some of the needs currently met by Israel. Palestinian imports from Israel run to as much as $2.3bn worth per annum. Of this, possibly some $400m worth could be transferred to Jordanian suppliers in short order. Among the raw materials which could be bought from Jordan instead of Israel are cement, fuel, fertilizer and flour. Equally, Palestinians could purchase more of their electrical goods from across the river. In all these instances, there would be a potential saving in terms of price – at least in theory. In practice there is a mark-up of over 100 per cent on goods from Jordan as a result of the logistical problems of transporting them via the bridge crossings, as discussed in Chapter 4.

A comparison of the Jordanian and Palestinian economies reveals more similarities than contrasts. Up to a point, similarity, especially in terms of culture and business practices, is a prerequisite for cooperation. However, complementarity is also required if both are to thrive rather than suffer from free trade. There are similarities between Jordan and Palestine in terms of types of agriculture and manufacturing industries; the structure of the labour force; education and skill levels; a common business culture, as well as language and religion; and a high degree of dependence on foreign aid.

As things stand, there are obstacles to expanding trade at all levels. The authorities on both sides of the river have to make political calculations about the relative effects of open borders on different sectors of their communities. Protectionism would not exist were it

---

7 A formula for doing this was posited in a paper produced by CSS in 1996 entitled, similarly to the survey produced the previous year, *The Jordanian–Palestinian Relationship: 'The Domestic Dimension'*.

not for the desire to shield certain sectors and members of the community from potential ruin. There are also vested interests firmly entrenched in both economic systems. Some of these are resistant to change. Others stand to gain from access to wider markets. Meanwhile, the whole subject of Jordanian–Palestinian economic relations is complicated by lack of information and clarity about where and how the costs and advantages of increased trade would take effect – at the state level, at the sectoral level, or at the level of individual companies and businesses. A beginning has been made, however, to collect data on these issues. For example, the Palestinian Economic Council for Development and Reconstruction (PECDAR) produced a study in 1996 on the pharmaceutical, shoemaking and clothing industries, comparing the competitive advantages of different sectors in the two communities. Certainly, such exercises are needed to determine what greater economic integration would actually mean.

As it is, all assessments of the prospects of Jordanian–Palestinian economic cooperation suggest that in the short term some will definitely suffer. The worst thing that could happen to the West Bankers would be unimpeded access for Jordanian agricultural products. For their part, Jordan's industrialists could suffer from greater Palestinian competition if all constraints were removed. Yet this assumes that competition would take place along national lines. In fact, joint ventures and cross-border investment could cut across the state divide, leading to competition between ventures, but not necessarily between the national sectors and economies. There is room for joint operations in tourism, transport, banking, manufacturing and agriculture, which would all benefit from the enlarged market. After an initial shake-down, during which non-competitive businesses would fall by the wayside, both economies would benefit from a more vibrant business environment. Yet this, of course, assumes that the state sector on both sides, plus the Israelis, can allow market forces to take their course.

The key to overcoming some of the obstacles clearly lies in the adoption of coordinated approaches to economic development on both sides of the river. Yet here the Israeli factor comes into play. Increased economic integration between Jordan and Palestine obviously has consequences for Israeli political and security interests. Commercial interests in Israel may also stand to lose out. The West Bank, as Gaza, has been a captive market for Israel. For this combination of reasons, Israel has adopted a stance in the negotiation of all the new economic agreements which ensures it a measure of control.

In the meantime, the popular mood in the West Bank has shifted palpably towards wanting more trade with Jordan, to substitute for some existing Israeli ties. On the Jordanian side, public opinion is 70 per cent in favour of Palestinian statehood across the river, which is not contradictory to interest in cooperation. These factors ought to facilitate moves to increase the economic viability of Palestine. Meanwhile, if economic isolation from both Israel and Jordan is inconceivable for Palestine, for Jordan economic development requires nurturing trading links with all its neighbours.

Turning to the question of infrastructures, there are several persuasive arguments for linking those of Jordan and Palestine. The geographic proximity of the two entities is obvious and there are no major physical obstacles, such as high mountains or deserts. The distances between their main business and economic centres are no more than a few tens of kilometres. The standards in operation for electrical power supplies are similar on both sides of the river. Also, cost considerations make duplication of facilities positively extravagant.

All infrastructure projects are high-investment undertakings, usually requiring 7–12 per cent of GNP of any national economy for a normal pace of growth. In Palestine, because of total neglect hitherto, anything less than a commitment of 20 per cent of GNP would imply very slow progress in the near term. In other words, massive new infrastructure building could not be synchronized with natural economic growth there. Moreover, growth depends on an adequate infrastructure and the lead time involved is quite long – three to four years in the case of a power station and four to five for a railway system. To start from scratch, Palestine clearly faces a problem in laying the basis for rapid economic development.

In some parts of the world, notably Southeast Asia, governments have chosen to phase in the introduction of infrastructure. In the Middle

East, however, infrastructure projects such as airports, ports and telecommunications are taken as symbols of sovereignty. Chauvinism tends to get in the way of sound economic sense. The average radius for airports in relation to capital cities is 90 km. Judged by this criterion, Jordan's airport facilities could readily serve Palestine too, or at least the West Bank. Impediments to crossing Israel probably mean that Gaza does need its own air and sea ports. Thus, in the Palestinian case, there is a need to juggle two imperatives: relative cost and freedom of manoeuvre. Cooperation with Jordan would seem to be the answer because (a) it makes economic sense for both partners, and (b) it means less reliance on Israel, for which security concerns are increasingly overriding all other considerations.

The discussions that informed the study presented here identified certain facets of Jordanian–Palestinian economic relations which demand urgent attention in the name of long-term economic benefit for both. These include:[8]

- *Roads and bridges*. These are inadequate for requirements. In particular, a new structure to replace the existing Allenby bridge between the West Bank and Jordan is needed to carry more traffic and vehicles of greater weight. Without it there cannot be increased trade. Plans are supposedly in place for this and external funding pledged, if only the parties, Israel included, can agree on the security logistics. Ease of passage for people must also be improved. At the moment, because of the interminable bureaucratic procedures and unloading and reloading from one vehicle to another, a journey from Jerusalem to Amman can take six hours. From Gaza, because of additional checkpoints, it takes twelve hours. Given the actual distances involved, it should take no more than about one hour from Jerusalem by car, and two and a half hours starting from Gaza.
- *Electrical power*. Progress has been painfully slow in this respect, and it is not clear which of the parties is principally to blame, though Israel is clearly the beneficiary of present arrangements. The Jordanian power lines run close to the Jordan Valley and it would only take a

---

[8] Data based on a workshop presentation by Ibrahim Badran.

few extra kilometres of lines to traverse the river. The Jordanian power station has a capacity of 1,000–1,100 megawatts, but the maximum demand in Jordan has been around 750 megawatts, so the surplus could be directed to Palestine. (Gaza needs a capacity of about 200 megawatts and the West Bank presumably needs twice that.) This would serve immediate needs; if another power station is envisaged, it could be built in Palestine, but as part of a joint network serving Jordan too. Jordan is already linked up to Syria and has plans to connect up to Egypt, and it makes no sense to start a separate arrangement for Palestine. Also, a Jordanian–Palestinian link-up would not rule out incorporating Israel into the regional grid too. So the proposal is not specifically directed against Israel, but in keeping with a vision of greater regional economic integration.

- *Water.* There are at present no joint water projects between Jordan and Palestine. The most logical way forward for them both to overcome their water shortage problems is cooperation on desalination plants, recycling and development of indigenous expertise. Israel has the lead in terms of technical know-how in this area, but this should not prevent further Jordanian–Palestinian cooperation.
- *Regional communications.* Geographically, it makes sense to link up the Gulf states and Iraq with the Mediterranean through Jordan and Palestine. Pipeline and railway connections traversing the region would facilitate a new economic order. Pending better political relations between the players concerned, Jordan and Palestine could at least prepare the way.

The triangular dimension

The Israeli response to Jordanian–Palestinian *Cooperation* would not necessarily be positive. As defined here, *cooperation under present circumstances* would be designed to bolster the Palestinian case for independent statehood, at least in the first instance. Anything beyond that is presaged on the prior establishment of an independent Palestinian state. This is a very different goal to the so-called 'Jordanian option' implicit in the *Functional* scenario. Consequently, *Cooperation* as depicted in this scenario would be likely to meet opposition from a hardline

Israeli government. It would cut across any Israeli agenda to recruit Jordanian complicity in containing Palestinian aspirations and power, and Jordanian collaboration on security in the Jordan Valley.

If a hardline Israeli government set about undermining the Palestinian Authority and Yasser Arafat's position, as posited under the *Functional* scenario, it could of course trigger precisely the kind of crisis that might persuade both the Palestinian and Jordanian leaders to reappraise the relative merits of cooperation. However, there is plenty of fertile ground to exploit in the mutual suspicions of the Palestinian president and King Hussein, should an Israeli leadership wish to sabotage *Cooperation*.

Conversely, there could be an Israeli constituency for Jordanian–Palestinian *Cooperation* as a mechanism for relieving some of the pressure on Israel to nanny the Palestinian economy, if not its political system, towards viability. Palestinian bomb attacks on Israelis have reinforced the Israeli constituency for separation from the Palestinians. The cumulative effect of Israeli security policies such as the 'closure' strategy could convince the Palestinians to look eastwards for more cooperation. In view of these trends, some Israelis could see benefits for regional stability if the Jordanians and Palestinians were to act in concert rather than competition.

Similar arguments will pertain to Israeli reactions to the prospect of some form of merger in the future. Those Israelis who used to claim, before the peace treaty with Jordan, that 'Jordan is Palestine' wanted to rid themselves of the Palestine problem by making Jordan the answer. Such elements would not regard a confederation, federation or union linking both banks of the Jordan as at all preferable. Any of these arrangements would fly in the face of the aspirations of 'Greater Israel' ideologues for Israeli annexation of the West Bank. On security grounds, meanwhile, Israelis might worry about the strength that such a Jordanian–Palestinian system could muster.

That said, Jordanian–Palestinian *Cooperation*, to the extent even of merger, need not rule out cooperation with Israel too. The Benelux model has some supporters as a possible scenario for the triangular relationship. Alternatively, some Israelis could see Jordanian–Palestinian *Cooperation* as the necessary prerequisite for achieving maximum separation from the Palestinians. Among these would be Israeli advocates of Palestinian statehood on ideological and security grounds (discussed in Chapter 3), who could see a link-up with Jordan as a form of guarantee for moderation.

Of all the possible outcomes for Israeli–Palestinian relations examined in Chapter 1, the one which fits most comfortably with the Jordanian–Palestinian *Cooperation* scenario is the *Beilin-Abu Mazen* formula. Without a contiguous border with Jordan it would be much more difficult for free trade, joint infrastructure arrangements and other forms of economic interchange to operate, let alone flourish. To achieve something approaching merger without a common border would be even more difficult.

The regional and international setting

A possibility of Jordanian–Palestinian and Israeli cooperation ought to meet with US approval. Given America's assessment of Jordan as a stable and dependable player in the region and its more sceptical appraisal of the Palestinian system, the linking of one to the other, with Israeli cooperation, could be viewed favourably. By the same token, however, other Arab states would probably not welcome the prospect of a Jordanian–Palestinian *confederation*, *federation* or *union*, because of the increased strength this new entity would represent, the expectation that it would come under Israeli influence and the blessing it might enjoy from the international community. For fear of this prospect in the region, various Arab players might choose to exploit sources of Jordanian–Palestinian friction to try to sabotage the endeavour.

Implications and outcomes

Of all the scenarios explored in this study, *Cooperation* will face the most obstacles and could well be the least likely to occur. However, it represents the antidote or remedy to the dangers implicit in the other scenarios. *Drift*, by definition, satisfies none of the parties to the peace process and courts the collapse of that process, with a violent fall-out.

Separation will throw Palestine on the mercy of Israel without the assistance of Jordan, while the *Functional* scenario appears to be unsustainable for the long term unless supplanted by deliberate *Cooperation*.

Here the implications of the scenario are discussed in conjunction with the various outcomes, for the sake of clarity, given that there are five permutations to the scenario. If what follows begins to sound like prescription rather than purely neutral description, this is probably because a certain amount of vision is required to depict what would be required to overcome the obstacles which have hitherto impeded cooperation.

(i) Cooperation under present circumstances

As of autumn 1997, *cooperation under present circumstances* implies reaching a common vision on final status issues and mutual support in dealing with third parties, not least the Israelis. It means, therefore, coordination and cooperation on Jerusalem, the issues of refugees, borders, Israeli settlements and security arrangements. It would be more effective if there were coordination on the question of normalization with Israel too, pending resolution of final status issues.

Because of historical, geographic, demographic and political considerations, both parties would have to be less sensitive about getting involved in each other's affairs. This could mean Transjordanians acknowledging a Palestinian dimension to Jordanian identity, and, by way of reciprocation, the Palestinian leadership could concede that Jordan has an interest in the Palestinian entity, and that both Jordanians and Palestinians in Jordan are affected by and concerned with day-to-day developments in Palestine.

One of the mechanisms for achieving the goal of *cooperation under present circumstances* would be the involvement of Jordanians and Palestinians at a number of levels in working out the parameters of cooperation. To effect political cooperation at the official level there could be a set of permanent committees meeting regularly and working in parallel, which would have to be qualitatively different from the kinds of talking shops often set up in the name of cooperation around the

Arab world. The involvement of experts with both a substantive knowledge of the issues and a commitment to the goal of cooperation would help. To illustrate, there could be four separate committees set up as follows:

(a) a higher coordinating committee, set up at the leadership level, for decision-making, exchanging information and policy coordination;
(b) a committee of parliamentarians from both sides to air differences and compare objectives;
(c) a committee of lawyers to examine the two legal systems and frameworks for incompatibilities and contradictions;
(d) a negotiations committee to coordinate on the details of Jordanian and Palestinian positions with regard to final status issues.

More informally, cooperation would be facilitated by the opening up to each other of civil society organizations on both sides. The fact that a number of such organizations in Jordan already integrate Jordanians and Palestinians in their memberships and activities could help pave the way.

The arrangements thus far described would set the scene for cooperation at the economic level. The objectives in this respect would be likely to include: bilateral free trade and a unified customs system; water-sharing agreements and desalination projects; capitalization on existing infrastructure arrangements for electricity supply, oil refineries, communications, transport, air and sea ports. Joint banks and project funds could facilitate joint business ventures. There could be expanded cooperation on tourism. Perhaps most importantly, there would have to be an agreed formula for the movement of labour and entitlements to residency. Because, in the short term, there could be at least as many losers as beneficiaries from economic cooperation, meeting the goals in this field would be extremely difficult and Israeli objections would have to be overcome too. Progress would probably be incremental and patchy at best.

In the interests of trying to bring all sectors of the two communities along with the endeavour, it would make sense to aim for cooperation on security concerns such as crime, smuggling and the black market. If this effort could be broadened to encompass coordination between security personnel on political violence and external security, it might be possible to develop this into a mechanism for ameliorating Israeli objections to facets of *Cooperation*. For practical reasons, too, there could be more bilateral dialogue and coordination on health, education and the environment.

In all these respects, the intention would presumably be to enhance the development of the Palestinian system, while also deriving some benefits for Jordan. The formally stated objectives of *cooperation under present circumstances* cannot include aspirations to some form of merger, since that would jeopardize attainment of even modest goals. Rather, the intention would be to pave the way for *cooperation between two states* because both sides would be cooperating in the name of achieving Palestinian statehood. However, unlike under the *Separation* scenario, the potential for something approaching merger in the future would not have been systematically undermined. All options would be open.

(ii) Coordination between two states

This version of the scenario would depend on Israeli acquiescence in the realization of Palestinian statehood in the West Bank and Gaza. It could mean Israeli–Palestinian negotiations resulting in a *Fifty-Fifty* solution (assuming the Palestinians could be persuaded to accept this), the *Beilin–Abu Mazen* formula or something in between.

In practice, *coordination between two states* would follow a similar pattern to *cooperation under present circumstances*, except that the framework of committees for cooperation on specific items would be headed by the two governments of the separate states. Also, since presumably the final status issues would have to have been resolved in the establishment of a Palestinian state with Israeli agreement, it would no longer be necessary to coordinate positions on these issues. In the event that *cooperation under present circumstances* had been achieved, prior to Palestinian independence, the resolution of the final status issues would presumably have involved all three members of the Jordan-

Palestine-Israel triangle, and the path to coordination and cooperation thereafter would have been smoothed.

That said, this version of the scenario obviously does not depend on the realization of *cooperation under present circumstances*. The two states could begin coordination from scratch, after Palestinian independence. However, if a trend towards the *Separation* scenario had become entrenched by then, whether by design or default, it would take more serious effort to establish a pattern of *coordination between two states* and the incentives to make such an effort might be lacking.

(iii) Cooperation approaching merger

None of the three versions of *cooperation approaching merger* described here are expected to come about without the prior attainment of Palestinian independence. Table 2 below encapsulates the basic features of the three models concerned.

(a) Confederation: Given the establishment of a Palestinian state, cooperation between Palestine and Jordan could take the form of a confederation between two states. The two governments would be linked by a treaty and various coordinating bodies, possibly a higher confederal council. There would probably be a single market and unified customs, alongside two currencies and two budgets. The arrangements for passports under this confederation could involve one national identity card plus local cards, or simply two separate passports.

(b) Federation: Cooperation in the form of a federation between Jordan and Palestine implies more shared institutions, as in one national parliament, together with two local ones; one constitution and two local governments; one currency and one federal budget, plus local budgets, and so on, as encapsulated in Table 2.

(c) Unity: Cooperation to the extent of unity would imply unification of all government institutions, the armed forces, the economy and so on, as also elaborated in Table 2.

Table 2

Cooperation scenarios between Jordanian and Palestinian states: a comparison

	Confederation	Federation	Unity
Constitution	Two national constitutions Treaty (linking two sides) Independent national laws	One constitution Local laws	One constitution
Parliament	Two national parliaments Joint parliament with limited authority	One national parliament Two local parliaments	One national parliament
Executive	Two governments Higher Confederal Council	One federal government Two local governments Federal Council, headed by the monarch and two prime ministers/appointed or elected	One government A democratic state with an elected president
Army and Security	Joint forces and security Separate special forces for each entity	One federal army	One army
Economy	One market, unified customs Two currencies Two budgets	One market, unified customs One currency One federal budget Local budgets	One economic system
Citizenship and Passport	One national card Local Identity cards Two passports	One passport Local identity cards	One passport One identity card
Sovereignty	Two sovereignties	One sovereignty	One sovereignty
Borders	Open borders	Without borders	Without borders

Confederation, federation or unity, as envisaged here, will require a consensus between and protections for both parties. Probably the only way this could come about is if all the alternatives look like destroying the prospects for peace and stability of both.

Note on Jerusalem

Cooperation under present circumstances would mean more Jordanian–Palestinian consultation on Jerusalem, but King Hussein would be likely to retain his role, as recognized by the Israelis, pending their agreement to a formal Palestinian role. Under all the other permutations of the *Cooperation* scenario, it may be assumed that Palestine would take on whatever sovereign and/or political rights the Israelis could be persuaded to concede.

6 CONCLUSIONS AND FUTURE IMPERATIVES

The intention has been to create four scenarios which are recognizably plausible and thereby underline the point that choices are available. Neither prediction nor prescription was intended, though elements of both may be discernible in the discussion. In fact, judging by events in the run-up to publication, the signs of *Cooperation* have been less in evidence than *Separation*, and the *Drift* and *Functional* scenarios provide more fitting explanations for developments during the course of 1997 than the other two. This could be because the *Drift* and *Functional* scenarios do not expect the Jordanians and Palestinians to take charge of their future relations; *Separation* requires a certain amount of effort but happens to fit with the goals of the Palestinian leadership and could come camouflaged as the quest for independence anyway; while *Cooperation* would require a deliberate act of will on both sides.

To summarize: the *Drift* scenario depicts what transpires if the Jordanian and Palestinian leaderships, along with the Israeli government, are in reactive mode, responding to events, not directing them. All the players engage in tactical manoeuvres, but none of them can impose a broad strategy. In Palestine the leadership could be preoccupied with consolidating power and moving further down the road to statehood, before tackling the question of relations with Jordan. If the peace process is going nowhere, that in itself will be a central concern. Other elements in society, from the elite to the street, will also focus more on the struggle for independence from Israel than on relations across the river. For their part, the Jordanians could prefer not to preempt developments on the Israeli–Palestinian track and therefore could simply stand on the sidelines voicing support for Palestinian statehood. Frustrations will presumably rise if there is no progress in

Arab–Israeli peace-making – which seems probable if the Israeli government is paralysed by internal divisions and power plays. The United States could also be immobilized by internal rivalry between the Democratic administration and the Republican congress, with neither wishing to antagonize Israel. Consequently, there will probably be no decisive intervention from abroad.

The outcome of *Drift* in Jordanian–Palestinian relations would be neither positive nor negative. Familial, material and psychological ties which bind the two peoples will persist along with the mutual suspicions and frictions. However, crisis could ensue if Israeli–Palestinian negotiations themselves drift towards total *Breakdown*, with renewed violence on the West Bank that could spill over into Jordan along with a new wave of refugees.

Each outcome for Jordanian–Palestinian relations has been correlated to one for Israeli–Palestinian relations, as indicated in Table 3. Since Jordan, Palestine and Israel are effectively locked into a triangle of interdependence, or one strategic space, as it has been termed here, developments in one dimension will obviously affect the others. That said, it would be wrong to concede to the peace process, or lack of it, the power to dictate Jordanian–Palestinian relations, unless both the Arab players are sucked into an Israeli agenda.

Such an eventuality underlies the *Functional* scenario. In this case, a hardline Israeli government such as that headed by Prime Minister Netanyahu is assumed to take the initiative, allowing the Palestinians no more than *Autonomy-Plus* in the West Bank. Neither the Palestinian nor the Jordanian leadership could endorse such an outcome. However, if the former is systematically marginalized and the latter finds itself filling the resulting power vacuum, albeit informally, the result could be a functional division of labour between the Israelis, the Palestinians and the Jordanians. Pressure, possibly sweetened with economic inducements could be brought to bear on Jordan from Israel and the United States. Even so, this scenario portends instability. It would be difficult for either the Jordanian or the Palestinian economy to overcome lack of investor confidence. Palestinian nationalism will retain its supporters on both sides of the

Jordan. The Islamists could gain in strength and a new generation of Fateh activists could become more assertive on the West Bank. Meanwhile, Transjordanian nationalists would resist deeper Jordanian involvement in political and economic affairs across the river, and would therefore become more vocal and possibly disruptive.

The *Separation* scenario takes developments in a very different direction from the *Functional* one. In fact, it may be driven by aversion to the very possibility of Jordanian involvement on the West Bank. It could come about as the by-product of the quest for Palestinian independence from Israel. As developed here, however, it assumes a Palestinian leadership determined to establish a political, legal and economic system as separate and distinct from that of Jordan as possible. Fateh could be expected to go along with this and the Islamists would find it hard to oppose it if it were camouflaged by the struggle for sovereignty. Similarly, public opinion in Jordan might not discern anything amiss with *Separation* if it were packaged in this way. One of the implications of this scenario, however, is that the Palestinian economy would end up more heavily dependent on Israel. In fact, by deliberately severing links with Jordan, the Palestinians would be more isolated in their dealings with Israel and their chances of realizing statehood would still rest on Israeli acquiescence. As explored in this study, the outcome of Israeli–Palestinian negotiations most compatible with Jordanian–Palestinian *Separation* is the *Fifty-Fifty* formula for a truncated Palestinian state, cut off from Jordan and surrounded by Israeli-controlled areas.

The *Cooperation* scenario represents a vision for Jordanian–Palestinian relations which would maximize the benefits to be gained from the two systems working in tandem. This would avoid the disadvantages of *Separation* and the instability and resentment inherent in the *Functional* scenario. Because mutual suspicions are so pronounced, however, the only way these could be overcome would be for *Cooperation* to be based on independent Palestinian statehood as a prerequisite. There could be *Cooperation under present circumstances* as a mechanism for enhancing the strength of both Palestine and Jordan in the triangular relationship with Israel. Those elements with vested interests in separation would present obstacles. The distrust between the two leaderships would be a major stumbling block which could only be overcome by a leap of the imagination. Probably, it would take a crisis in Jordanian–Palestinian relations to make this possible. Once achieved, however, cooperation in the near term could smooth the path for something more adventurous in the long run. Judging by opinion poll data collected on either side of the Jordan, though, a perception of a special relationship exists alongside Palestinian and Transjordanian fears of closer mutual involvement. To work best, *Cooperation* would sit most comfortably with an outcome to Israeli–Palestinian negotiations along the lines of the *Beilin-Abu Mazen* plan.

This brief summary can in no way substitute for the full exploration of the four scenarios provided in this study. Also, it is important to remember that the idea of developing alternative scenarios was devised as a response to the difficulties which prevent Jordanians and Palestinians from agreeing on how to cooperate to mutual benefit. The work which informed this study was a collaborative endeavour between Jordanian and Palestinian specialists from both sides of the Jordan. Their humour and enthusiasm for the task helped smooth the way through heated debates about mutual suspicions and historical animosities. The whole process was in itself a reflection of the special relationship. The end result was productive because the participants agreed to focus on achievable objectives instead of trying to resolve all their outstanding differences.

The agreed objective which emerged was to provide an impetus to more constructive thinking by Palestinians and Jordanians in general about their future relations and to depart from a tendency to let events dictate their fates. It is because of this tendency that the *Drift* and the *Functional* scenarios are so plausible. The *Separation* scenario has credibility because distrust and rivalry could drive the two sides apart. Yet *Cooperation* is not wholly beyond the bounds of possibility because it is a logical response to outside pressures as well as mutual interests. What has been lacking is reciprocal recognition of the legitimate interests of each side in the future stability of the other. As has been discussed, however, it will take an effort of will, and probably a further deterioration in relations, before the logical imperatives stemming from interdependence can be fully recognized and constructively embraced.

Meanwhile, it is hoped that this study will help to lift debate to a new level. It is the intention of the partner institutes which have produced it to undertake more research on the implications of each scenario and to look specifically at ways of bringing about Jordanian–Palestinian cooperation in terms of legal arrangements affecting trade and political rights and freedoms; currency circulation and controls; infrastructure building; education; and the issues of passports and residency rights. As with the scenario-building exercise, the objective will be to define choices based on relevant information.

As this study goes to press, the chances for a breakthrough in Israeli–Palestinian negotiations do not look promising. Equally, it seems all too likely that either *Drift* or the *Functional* scenario will come about, infused with an unrealized impetus towards *Separation*. Consequently, it seems appropriate to conclude here with a table relating the scenarios for Jordanian–Palestinian relations to those for Israeli–Palestinian relations. This aims to provoke thinking about how inaction or short-sightedness in the former relationship could increase the likelihood of certain outcomes in the latter.

Table 3

Jordan / Palestine \ Israel / Palestine	Beilin-Abu Mazen	Fifty/fifty	Autonomy-Plus	Drift
Plausible combinations of Jordanian–Palestinian and Israeli–Palestinian scenarios					
Cooperation	X			
Separation		X		
Functional			X	
Drift				X

X – Most plausible combination